Human rights must be unconditionally respected.

I0441333

Book content:

Prologue

Respect for human rights is a necessity and obligation of each State and citizen of the planet.

Violation of human rights by States can lead to great social conflicts.

Unfortunately, many states still do not respect human rights.

Prevents human rights crisis.

Human rights must be made known to people they know and if not satisfied ask to be respected.

Respect for human rights contribute greatly to creating and maintaining social harmony.

The right of every citizen of the planet must be respected by each state and the citizens.

Universal Declaration of Human Rights UN (United Nations) must be made known to every citizen of the world and be met by institutions of countries that have signed it.

Respecting human rights can be made more progress in many areas.

Respect for human rights without much trouble, suffering, unhappiness, abuse, injustice, discrimination, inequity, tragedies, much poverty, high unemployment, sickness mass of billions of people.

Every citizen of the planet has the right and obligation to fight for human rights in the world, in every country.

Citizens of the world can make progress more rapid and greater respect for human rights if it will hold much better in non-profit organizations, NGOs, national and international human rights.

AGC ideas and thoughts in this book and others that come directly and indirectly contribute to the formation of a global consciousness for human rights, the thinking, ideas, action and positive behaviors in each of us.

Please write me how you have helped these ideas.

The money invested in this book of mine and the others that follow it is worth it, and it is almost nothing comparing to the pozitive efects that this book can have in your life, by applying the ideas to your life.

This volumes must be bought and used day by day, in order to development your personality and to the accomplish of all that you want.

These books contain lots of pozitive, optimist, creative, dinamic ideas, that push you to action, to thinking, things that are necesary your daily life and to accomplish your personal objectives.

Reading and analizing the ideas in this book and aplying them, we'll fiind solutions and ideas that will help us find:

I. To discover:

1. Qualities

2. Defects

3. Capabilities

4. Qualifications

5. Some opportunities to succeed in life

6. Feelings

7. What we do to be loved

8. How to love

9. How to realize and maintain a true mutual love

10. How to realize and maintain a happy marriage

11. mistakes, errors, wrong ideas

12. Etc.

II. To prevent some:

1. Divorces

2. Mistakes

3. Suspect

4. Griefs

5. Conflicts

6. Accidents

7. Failures

8. Bankrupstcy

9. Etc.

III. To become more:

1. Happy

2. Loved

3. Honored,

4. Appreciated,

5. Wanted,

6. Optimistic,

7. Good,

8. Unselfish,

9. Emotional,

10. Altruists

11. Stronger

12. Efficient

13. Organized

14. Planners

15. Active

16. Honest

17. Human

18. Popular

19. Famous

20. Flexible

21. Adaptable

22. Understanding

23. Prompt

24. Etc.

IV. To get out of a state of:

    1. Despair

    2. Pessimism

    3. Passiveness

    4. Inactivity

    5. Inefficiency

    6. Inflexibility

    7. Crisis

    8. Inadaptability

    9. Etc.

V. To participate more actively to:

    1. Social life

    2. Political life

    3. Nonprofit organizations activities

    4. Etc

VI. To participate more actively and efficiently in achieving true love and a happy marriage

VII. To find more likely situations conducive to achieving and maintaining a happy marriage life

VIII. To change our life for the better and to make It more beautiful

IX. To multiply and increase the chances to find your life partner

X. To raise and educate our children better so we can take better care of them

XI. Fiind more and bigger chances to meet favourable situations to accomplish and maintain a happy marriage for life.

XII. Change our life in good and make it better.

XIII. To multiply and increase the chances to find your life partner

XIV. To raise and educate our children better so we can take better care of them

I write and gather these thoughts, ideas in books, internet and other publications because these are useful to us every day and it is necessary to apply them to accomplish what we want, a better and beautiful life and propsperous.

These thoughts reflect a small part of what is good in reality and human relationships.

I wait to hear from you good news, good deeds that you have done influenced from what you have read from these books to make your life more beautiful, properous, happier and to be a pozitive example for others.

Each of us an become pozitive examples for others around us, participating to the creation of a better, prosperous and happier human society.

I'd be happy if one or more ideas read from these books helped you in a way or another and made you happier and prosperous.

I'm waiting to hear from you, your ideas and oppinions, your joys and griefes and your suggestions for new book subjects and i also appeal to your participation of promoting on the internet and mass media of the ideas and the books i've written.

I invite you to e-mail me at my email address: agcornel@gmail.com.

Dear readers I wish you all health, happiness and achievement of all your wishes.

Best regards and respect,

Gheorghe Cornel Ardelean

981 Principal Street
Macea, Arad county
Zip Code 371210
Romania
Tel # (40)-0788-725-204
(40)-0788-725-913

Abuse

1. Injustice is also an abuse.

2. Societies make abuses when they do not protect the helpless.

3. Societies make "n" abuses against the unprotected, by not protecting them.

4. The society makes "n" abuses against the unprotected, by not protecting them.

5. A judge makes a lesser mistake if he gives a smaller sentence than to abuse and be wrong so as to give an illegally bigger punishment.

6. Women are mostly abused in family violence.

7. Not respecting human rights is a serious abuse done by states.

8. Not respecting the right to nondiscrimination of people by the state is a great abuse.

9. Not assuring personal freedom is a great abuse.

10. Constructive thinking makes us have zero tolerance towards abuse.

11. All types of abuse in society can and must be prevented in time.

12. Any abuse may cause another or other abuse.

13. The law must prevent any possible abuse.

14. Abuse must be prevented by law.

15. Abuse must be discouraged by the law.

16. Many times abuse causes many negative effects.

17. Most abuses can be prevented with the help of an effective law.

Accept

18. Although many scientific researches have found that smoking damages very much our health, even that of those who are non-smokers, all countries accept the legal industry and related trade of cigarettes, which cause tens and hundreds of millions of illnesses and deaths. The situation is incredible, but unfortunately, it exists in all of the world's states. Why do we even tolerate such incredibly damageable activities for

billions of people, with incalculable negative effects?

19.   He who brutal is not accepted by most people.

20.   There are people who do not accept jokes.

21.   My meditations give us an impulse to achieve our personal goals. Read, analyze them and apply those you accept. Good luck.

22.   My meditations push us, give us impulses to do only what is good for us, for others, and for society. Read, analyze them and apply those you accept. Good luck.

23.   My meditations push us, give us impulses to achieve a better life. Read, analyze them and apply those you accept. Good luck.

24.   My meditations push us, give us impulses to take care of us, of our health, of our family etc. Read, analyze them and apply those you accept. Good luck.

25.   My meditations push us, give us impulses to do what is necessary and required. Read, analyze them and apply those you accept. Good luck.

26. My meditations push us, give us impulses to achieve a better world. Read, analyze them and apply those you accept. Good luck.

27. Thought my help you can prevent many mistakes. Read, analyze them and apply those you accept. Good luck!

28. Love for the vast majority of women is particularly important. Given this fact in having a relationship of true love, unfortunately, many facts are unacceptable.

29. Life without true love for many young people is unacceptable.

30. My meditations help us achieve and maintain a happy marriage. Read, analyze and apply those that you accept. Good luck.

31. My meditations help us achieve and maintain true love. Read, analyze and apply those that you accept. Good luck.

32. My meditations impulse us, push us to achieve and maintain a happy marriage. Read, analyze and apply those that you accept. Good luck.

33. My meditations impulse us and push us to achieve and maintain true love. Read,

analyze and apply those that you accept. Good luck.

34. My meditations impulse us, push us to succeed in life. Read, analyze and apply those that you accept. Good luck.

35. Some people call crazy all those who have ideas that they do not accept.

36. Lack of common sense is an unacceptable defect of any man.

37. Any act of family aggression, made by a family member against another member of the family can not be reasoned and legally bound to be accepted under any circumstances.

38. The one who is superficial in what he does is not accepted and employed by many employers.

39. Rudeness is an unacceptable defect.

40. Although rudeness is unacceptable in the XXI century, it is still too widespread.

41. Constructive thinking does not accept the non-abiding of human rights.

42. Arrogance between spouses is unacceptable.

43. Arrogance between friends is unacceptable.

44. Arrogance between lovers is unacceptable.

45. Each woman has the need to feel accepted.

Accuse

46. We have no right to accuse someone because we want to do so without having evidence.

47. To accuse someone intentionally in an illegal way is a crime.

48. He who is accused in bad faith, illegally, has long suffered unjustly.

49. The negative effects for that or those wrongly accused should be borne by the one or ones who have wrongly accused him and the proper moral damages should also.

50. Men, when they have failures, must not accuse the woman or their wife.

Aggression

51. Aggression leads to complicated problems, not to solving problems.

52. Any act of aggression against a family member by another family member is illegal and can be punished by the law.

53. The prevention of each member of a family of all acts of aggression against another member of his family should be continuously, day by day a personal goal.

54. Any potential act of aggression of one member by another family member can be prevented by the potential aggressor with calm, patience, forbearance, wisdom, etc..

55. Any act of aggression of one member by another family member leads to complicating the problems and in no case to resolve the problems.

56. The disparagement aggression of a member by another family member by society contributes greatly to preventing further aggression among the families and other families, society.

57. The family is necessary to prevent any situation of verbal aggression.

58. Verbal aggression in the family is a behavior that harms the family's happiness.

59. The support of a family member, by other members of his family, in order to prevent any act of aggression on the other family members is required to become a personal goal continuously, day by day, for as long as we live.

60. Any act of aggression of one member by another family member is inadmissible and can not be justified.

61. Any act of family aggression, made by a family member against another member of the family can not be reasoned and legally bound to be accepted under any circumstances.

62. Aggression is a result of ignorance.

63. Aggression is a survival of primitive times.

64. Aggression in the family must not be found.

65. In any case, no matter how difficult it would be, a family should never resort to aggression.

66. Verbal aggression in the family leads to the creation of psychological discomfort in the family.

67. Verbal aggression in the family is a primitive behavior.

68. Verbal aggression in the family is against the family.

69. Physical aggression in the family is a primitive behavior.

70. Physical aggression in the family does so much harm to the happiness of the family.

71. The prevention of every member of our families of aggressions against another family member in many cases prevents many divorces.

72. A family is necessary to prevent any situation of verbal aggression.

73. Verbal aggression in a family is a behavior that damages the happiness of the family.

74. Each family member should contribute as much as he can to prevent family aggressions in his family.

75. Many times, aggression produces much aggression.

76. We must not respond to aggression with aggression.

Aggressive

77. Men who are aggressive against a family member may change in behavior. Those who say they can not change in behavior and they will not be aggressive towards one of the members of his family are wrong.

78. Our hostile non aggressive behavior helps us become more operative.

79. Women who are aggressive against their family members may change their aggressive behavior to be a non-aggressive behavior in any family situation.

80. An aggressive behavior of the husband towards the wife is very harmful for children.

81. A non-hostile but aggressive behavior increases our potential of achieving personal goals.

82. A non-hostile but aggressive behavior helps us a lot to become more efficient.

83. A non-hostile but aggressive behavior helps us a lot in achieving outstanding performances.

84. A non hostile but aggressive behavior increases our chances and all our potential of achieving more and greater successes.

85. A non hostile but aggressive behavior helps us increase our credibility.

86. A non hostile but aggressive behavior helps us a lot to prevent many failures.

87. A non hostile but aggressive behavior helps us have more chances to meet more favorable situations.

88. A non-hostile but aggressive behavior helps us achieve efficient co operations.

Altruism

89. Altruism helps us create a happy marriage.

90. Altruism helps us achieve more easily more successess.

91. Altruism helps us greatly expand the chances to achieve effective co operations.

92. Altruism helps greatly expand our opportunities to achieve personal goals.

93. Altruism helps us greatly expand the chances to become happy.

94. Each parent is required to form and develop altruism in children.

95. Altruism helps us greatly increase our chances to achieve effective co operations.

96. Altruism helps us very much to increase our chances to achieve our personal goals.

97. Altruism greatly increases our chances to become happy.

98. Altruism helps us have more chances to achieve effective co operations.

99. Altruism helps us achieve a mature love.

100. Altruism helps us achieve a happy marriage.

101. Altruism helps us more easily achieve more successes.

102. Our transformation for the better can be achieved also through the formation, development, maintenance and usage of altruism.

Arrogance

103. Arrogance alienate sus from a lot of people.

104. Arrogance is a great flaw.

105. Arrogance can sometimes cause us much harm.

106. Arrogance leads to many conflicts.

107. Arrogance can be prevented.

108. Arrogance makes us be repugnant to some people.

109. Arrogance can create many failures in life.

110. Arrogance is a brake, is an obstacle to achieving many friendships.

111. Those who have high objectives in life mostly have the spirit of arrogance.

112. Arrogance between spouses is unacceptable.

113. Arrogance between friends is unacceptable.

114. Arrogance between lovers is unacceptable.

115. Arrogance is repelling.

116. Arrogance is very harmful to inter-human relationships.

Blame

117. When we make a mistake and we say others or another is to blame, we make another mistake.

118. When we are wrong we are to blame not other people.

119. It is necessary and we must self-impose not to blame others when another when we are wrong, but to analyze and find out why we are wrong.

120. When a love relationship breaks we must not seek to blame only the other.

121. Those who do not seek favorable circumstances think that everything is unfortunate; they are not looking for blame,

they are passive and wait for luck to fall from heaven.

122. Those who did not seek favorable situations say that everything is unfortunate that they are not looking to blame, they are passive and expect luck to come to them from haven.

123. Those who believe that others are to blame for their mistakes are illogical in that rationality.

124. The states in which those who have common sense are marked by those who do not have common sense are to blame and have the right and obligation to prevent such an abnormality.

125. The states in which only poverty exists are to blame for the existence of poverty.

Bitterness

126. Bitterness harms us.

127. We can prevent bitterness by thinking positively.

128. Bitterness is very harmful.

129. Bitterness must be prevented.

130. Bitterness can be prevented.

131. Prolonged bitterness is very harmful to our health.

132. The self-control of our behaviors helps us a lot to prevent bitterness.

Brutality

133. Brutality harm us very much.

134. Brutality is a negative behavior that we can prevent.

135. Brutality between spouses has no place.

136. The brutality between spouses enormously harms the marriage.

137. The brutality between spouses can be prevented.

138. Brutality removes us from others.

139. Brutality is a primitive behavior.

140. Brutality is an inefficiency of education.

Careless

141. We must avoid being careless.

142. Young people from all of the world's states should not be negligent, careless, passive, inactive, non-participative in taking decisions that concern them, their present and future, but to take part in decision-making in local councils, central parliaments, governments and other state and non-state institutions, and use all their capacities, abilities, skills, attitudes, knowledge, energy, commitment and desire to assert and achieve great deeds, to create a more humane, more righteous, more happy, with less trouble world.

143. Carelessness was often the cause of many failures.

144. Young people who are careless when their rights are unobserved make very big mistakes.

145. We should never be careless about injustice.

146. A man who is careless about himself and about others is dangerous.

147. A man who is careless and without objectives is a danger to himself.

Charitable

148. We can contribute to the achievement of our greatest accomplishments also through the contribution of the formation, development, maintenance and usage of charitable behavior.

149. Release from our self-imposed restrictions can be made also through the contribution of the formation, development, maintenance and usage of charitable behavior.

150. The force of our ideas can be augmented also through the contribution of the formation, development, maintenance and usage of charitable behavior.

151. We can become stronger and we can not allow ourselves to be influenced by the world also through the contribution of the formation, development, maintenance and usage of charitable behavior.

152. Self-imposed discipline helps us become charitable.

153. Rather than lamenting that we do not have successes it is more useful to also form, develop, maintain and use charitable behavior.

154. Pessimism can be removed and replaced with optimism also through the contribution of the formation, development, maintenance and usage of charitable behavior.

155. In order to rise up once again for the first time for the who knows what time it is necessary to also form, develop, maintain and use charitable behavior.

156. The obstacles that prevent us from achieving our personal goals can be surpassed also through the contribution of the formation, development, maintenance and usage of charitable behavior.

157. We can prevent the falling apart of a happy marriage also through the contribution of the formation, development, maintenance and usage of charitable behavior.

158. Hopes can be created also through the contribution of the formation, development, maintenance and usage of charitable behavior.

159. We can prevent some failures also through the contribution of the formation, development, maintenance and usage of charitable behavior.

160. In order to prevent failures it is necessary to also form, develop, maintain and use charitable behavior.

161. Continuous self-motivation helps us become charitable.

162. The radical transformation for the better of our life can be achieved also through the formation, development, maintenance and usage of charitable behavior.

Citizen

163. Abnormalities in each country can be replaced with normalities, as more citizens from those countries operate with more efficiency and devotion so that normalities take the place of abnormalities, where they exist.

164. States and international organizations have the right and obligation to create themselves conditions so that citizens can be able to handle jobs in which they are most effective and operational and it must reward them properly, in order to keep them in those positions.

165. The world' countries need and must take the necessary steps to create and develop every citizen's ability and creative thinking, because they are particularly important for each country and human in part, for the country's problems, the world's problems and the objectives of each man.

166. Member institutions, individuals, international organizations, nonprofit organizations, private firms, etc.. are necessary to carry out projects that lead to the positive use of knowledge of as many citizens of the world to achieve personal goals, whereas today it is basically used by very few people as compared to the world's population and very little knowledge of the existent one is used.

167. All the people on this earth have sufficient resources through their huge resources, by unity, solidarity, co operation, co-development, perseverence, will, work, Internet, media, etc. to install itself in a record time in many places and situations, abnormalities instead of the normal. Get started now as you will always succeed because you are an invincible force, you can replace abnormalities with normal situations

and places. Persevere until you succeed and if needed continually ask for the help of other citizens of the planet that you will be joined by incredibly many of them. Good luck. I am sure you will succeed.

168. Measures to prevent crime do not only reduce prison terms and large punishments with imprisonment, there are much more effective measures from all points of view including a citizen who spends large amounts of money because of the inefficient legal system based only on prison terms.

169. States should be concerned about citizens especially for an efficient education suitable to all intents and purposes that meet real needs of education of people and society so that both needs are effectively met.

170. Every citizen of the state is required to act in one way or another to contribute to enhancing the quality of the activities and actions of justice.

171. A journalist who knowingly, for some reward, misinforms private citizens has no moral right to be a journalist, but also because legally his facts are crimes.

172. Consummer's Protection is required to extend its powers to check the activities of all state institutions that provide public services to citizens.

173. Every citizen of the state is required to act in one way or another to contribute to enhancing the quality of court actions.

174. Not caring about the problems that regard us is an unfit behavior for a citizen.

175. People on earth have sufficient resources to unite their huge forces, through solidarity, cooperation, co-development, perseverance, willpower, work, the Internet, the media, the mobile phone, etc., to install in record time in many places and situations normality instead of abnormalities. Start right now that you will always succeed for you are an invincible force, you can replace the abnormal with the normal in no matter what situations and places. Persevere until you succeed and if you need it, continually ask for help from other citizens of the planet that will join you to become incredibly many. Good luck. I am sure you will succeed.

176. Measures to prevent crime not only reduce the pain of very high prison sentences, there

is a need for much more effective measures from all points of view inclusively for a citizen having to support large amounts of money because of an ineffective legal system of prison terms.

177. States need and must assure access to the Internet for all its citizens.

Control

178. We can become stronger and we can not allow ourselves to be influenced by the world also through the contribution of the formation, development, maintenance and usage of continuous control of the self behavior.

179. Pessimism can be removed and replaced with optimism also through the contribution of the formation, development, maintenance and usage of self-controlled behavior.

180. Continuous self-control helps us become persevering.

181. Continuous self-control helps us become animated.

182. Continuous self-control helps us become capable.

183. Will helps us become self controlled.

184. Continuous self-control helps us become decent.

185. Some mistakes can be prevented also through the contribution of the formation, development, maintenance and usage of continuous self-control behavior.

186. In order to prevent not achieving our personal goals, it is necessary to also form, develop, maintain and use our self-controlled behavior.

187. Continuous self-control helps us become ordered.

188. Continuous self-control helps us become audacious.

189. Wisdom helps us become self controlled.

190. Our resistance to changing for the better can be overcome also through the contribution of the formation, development, maintenance and usage of self-controlled behavior.

191. The radical transformation for the better of our life can be achieved also through the formation, development, maintenance and

usage of continuous control of the self behavior.

192. In order to stand up once again for the first time or for the who knows what time, it is necessary to also form, develop, maintain and use a self-controlled behavior.

193. Continuous self-control helps us become analytic.

194. We can prevent the falling apart of a happy marriage also through the contribution of the formation, development, maintenance and usage of continuous self-controlling behavior.

195. Continuous self-control helps us become optimistic.

196. Rather than lamenting that we do not have successes it is more useful to also form, develop, maintain and use a continuously control of the self behavior.

197. Continuous self-control helps us become initiating.

198. Continuous self-control helps us become harmless.

199. Stress can be prevented also through the formation, development, maintenance and usage of continuous self-controlling behavior.

200. Continuous self-control helps us become energetic.

201. Continuous self-control helps us become flexible.

202. We can prevent the falling apart of a happy marriage also through the contribution of the formation, development, maintenance and usage of self-controlled behavior.

203. Continuous self-control helps us become daring.

204. Aspiring towards a more meaningful life can also be achieved through the formation, development, maintenance and usage of continuous self-controlling behavior.

205. Continuous self-control helps us become selfless.

206. Continuous self-control helps us become trained.

207. Release from our self-imposed restrictions can be made also through the contribution of the formation, development, maintenance and usage of self-controlled behavior.

208. Continuous self perfection helps us become self-controlled.

209. Continuous self-control helps us become bold.

210. We can form, develop and maintain the state of being ourselves also through the contribution of the formation, development, maintenance and usage of a self-controlled behavior.

211. Continuous self-control helps us become fighting.

212. Continuous self-control helps us become self controlled.

213. Continuous self-control helps us become attachable.

214. Our resistance to changing for the better can be overcome also through the contribution of the formation, development, maintenance and usage of continuous self-control behavior.

215. Continuous self-control helps us become strong.

216. Continuous self-control helps us become organized.

217. Aspiring towards a more meaningful life can also be achieved through the formation, development, maintenance and usage of continuous control of the self behavior.

218. Continuous self-control helps us become cheerful.

219. The obstacles that prevent us from achieving our personal goals can be surpassed also through the contribution of the formation, development, maintenance and usage of continuous self-controlling behavior.

220. We can contribute to the achievement of our greatest accomplishments also through the contribution of the formation, development, maintenance and usage of continuous self-control behavior.

221. Continuous self-control helps us become firm.

222. Our own happiness can be achieved and maintained also through the contribution of the formation, development, maintenance and usage of self-controlled behavior.

223. Continuous self-control helps us become perfectionists.

224. Continuously making ourselves efficient helps us become self controlled.

225. Continuous self-control helps us become kind.

Crimes

226. Illiteracy is directly or indirectly the cause of many crimes.

227. Judges which during their professional activity have committed crimes should have the common sense to give their resignation themselves.

228. Unfortunately, many times no protection by the society of those who need it has enormously negative effects and multiple ones that are irreversible on them, sometimes resulting in suicides, deaths, self-mutilations, killings, physical and psychological damage, some irreversible,

crimes with many years of conviction, inhuman life under the open sky, on the streets, in suers, etc.

229. One of the causes of many crimes is also that generated by the fact that society has not provided, although it was necessary and obligatory, human protection for those who have committed certain crimes.

230. Many crimes could be prevented by preventing the causes that lead certain people to the need for human protection by providing human protection from society to people who have arrived in a position where they need it.

231. Unfortunately, society is not concerned enough, does not take the necessary measures to prevent the causes that lead certain people in a position where they need social protection and ensure the needed and obligatory human protection for people who need it.

232. In fact, through this inhuman, ineffective, irresponsible, illegal, selfish, abusive, etc. behavior, society, unfortunately, has a great contribution to the achievement of many crimes committed by people who needed

human protection and were not given any.

233. The systems, the formal measures of the state made to solve human problems, the judicial system with certain behaviors typical to slave-owning, feudal, totalitarian, communist, inhuman, against man etc. societies. Many times in many situations people can decay morally, degrade mentally and physically, degrade their health, be an expert in crimes.

234. Education that is inadequate is the direct or indirect cause of most crimes.

235. Inadequate education is a major cause of the very many crimes.

236. By conducting a proper education states can prevent many crimes.

237. They can prevent many crimes by taking effective measures to prevent crime for each type of crime.

238. It is necessary to immediately take the necessary measures to achieve an efficient education suitable to be able to prevent crime very much by this method, which

consists in carrying out an effective education appropriate to make people not want to commit crimes.

239. Some judges have done and made in their life, only through their participation in meetings of the court, more crimes than the total number of offenses prosecuted by them.

240. Unfortunately, there is a great number of lawyers who should be behind bars, because of the many crimes that they have done, and damage that they have done because of irregular relations with customers.

241. Ignorance is directly or indirectly the cause of most crimes.

242. Some behaviors, such as a negative mentality, can lead to crimes.

243. If you unfortunately have some negative mentalities (which may be crimes) is good to stop their use.

244. A journalist who knowingly, for some reward, misinforms private citizens has no moral

right to be a journalist, but also because legally his facts are crimes.

245. Unfortunately, a number of lawyers should be behind bars because of the many crimes they have done, because of the misfortunes and damage they have done, because of illegal behaviors in their relationship with their clients.

246. Some behaviors, called mentalities, are not in fact mentalities, but crimes.

247. If you unfortunately have some negative mentalities (which may be crimes) it is better to stop using them.

248. Wisdom prevents many crimes.

249. Inadequate education is directly or indirectly the cause of most crimes.

250. Ruses can help at the time not to be discovered, but after their discovery they could be extremely harmful, depending on the seriousness of the crimes and on the size of their negative effects.

251. Inadequate education is a major cause of many crimes.

252. By making a proper education states can prevent many crimes.

253. States can prevent many crimes if they take effective measures to prevent the crimes for every type of crime.

254. Since 2007 most states do not apply the appropriate measures for the most effective prevention of crimes, unfortunately, but they apply only primitive and inefficient methods of punishment through prison.

255. States need to take the immediate necessary measures to provide a proper education efficiency to be able to prevent many crimes by this method, which consists in carrying out an effective appropriate education for people who do not want to commit crimes.

256. Constructive thinking makes us have zero tolerance for crimes.

257. By preventing the formation of causes of crimes we prevent crime.

258. Crimes can be prevented.

259. The self-control of our behaviors helps us a lot to prevent some crimes.

Criminal

260. The judge who committed an injustice is necessary and required to answer criminaly, civilly, financialy, for that injustice.

261. Forming, developing and rewarding positive performance in children makes us not have performers in negative performance, namely criminals.

262. The one who has made an injustice is necessary to respond criminally and civilly for the injustice done.

263. Illegal actions lead us to prison. Warning. You can easily go to prison. Read the Criminal Code.

264. The judicial and criminal investigations must take place as peaceful as possible.

Cruelty

265. Cruelty is a primitive behavior.

266. Cruelty behavior is that of a man without a soul.

267. Cruelty surely removes others from those who are cruel.

268. Cruelty only has very large negative effects and never positive ones.

269. It is needed to prevent cruelty by as many effective measures as we can and especially through education since kindergarten.

Dangerous

270. Dehumanization is very dangerous to society.

271. Organized state crime is the most dangerous crime because it is conducted by officials of state and elected officials, other staff working for the state or on behalf of the state and they are using their function in avhieving the crime of using their function, institution and other institutions of the state.

272. Corruption is so generalized in the world and so harmful that it constitutes a global danger of humanity, the greatest and the most dangerous and with negative effects that it creates for society.

273. The man whom you can not trust is dangerous.

274. Hatred is extremely dangerous.

275. Revenge is extremely dangerous.

276. A man without judgement is extremely dangerous.

277. Stupidity is extremely dangerous.

278. Pettiness is extremely dangerous.

279. Waste is extremely dangerous.

280. Envy is a cancer, very dangerous, it eats us on the inside.

281. Discrimination is a very dangerous factor of stress.

282. He who is irrational is extremely dangerous.

283. The foolish man is extremely dangerous.

284. Artfulness is a very dangerous flaw.

285. The man who is sick is extremely dangerous.

286. Hypocrisy is extremely dangerous.

287. The man who does not even know what is good for him is extremely dangerous.

288. Boorishness is an extremely dangerous flaw.

289. The man who is irrational is extremely dangerous.

290. A man who is careless about himself and about others is dangerous.

291. Laziness a dangerous defect.

292. Laziness is a dangerous defect.

293. A lying man is extremely dangerous.

294. The man that you can not trust is dangerous.

295. Corrupt politicians are very dangerous; they are like viruses.

296. Human stupidity is incredibly dangerous most of the times.

Democracy

297. Democracy is one of the factors of human and social progress.

298. Freedom and democracy have also created more chances and opportunities for personal development.

299. Political corruption is a very great danger to democracy.

Destruction

300. The hypocrisy of a friend towards the other leads to the destruction of the friendship.

301. Senselessness in the relationship between spouses, if repeated, often leads to the destruction of the happy marriage.

302. Arguments often lead to the destruction of many happy marriages.

303. Premature actions around the world are done every day, unfortunately, causing enormously much trouble, misfortune, destruction, and much worse producing enormous damages.

304. Unconsidered words have led to the destruction of many friendships.

305. Misunderstandings in true friendships must never lead to the destruction of that friendship.

306. We must always do everything necessary to avoid the destruction of true friendship.

307. Repeated offenses between lovers can lead to the destruction of love.

308. Offenses between those who cooperate can lead to the destruction of the cooperation.

Development

309. Common people succeed in maintaining efficient co-developments.

310. Team spirit helps us achieve efficient co-developments.

311. The capacity of anticipating people's needs helps us maintain our efficient co-developments.

312. Very sociable and open persons have more chances of achieving efficient co-developments.

313. A strategic vision increases our chances of achieving efficient co-developments.

314. By doing the right thing we will succeed in achieving our necessary efficient co-developments.

315. A man sure of himself has great chances of achieving efficient co-developments.

316. The ability of reacting with understanding helps us a lot to achieve efficient co-developments.

317. A man with courage achieves efficient co-developments also.

318. Advanced education contributes a lot in achieving efficient co-developments.

319. Those who are preoccupied with creating on optimal cooperation in a team have the qualities and a much greater potential and chances to achieve efficient co-developments.

320. Efficient co-developments sometimes help us be lucky.

321. Those who know that discipline is one of the keys of dreams have the ability to maintain their desired efficient co-developments.

322. People who have the ability to react with understanding have more chances to maintain their efficient co-developments.

323. Persons who have no hopes, in order to create their hopes in the future, need to connect with people who participate in achieving efficient co-developments.

324. Hesitating behavior reduces the chances of achieving efficient co-developments.

325. The ability to adopt visions helps us a lot in achieving efficient co-developments.

326. Orientation towards a future world helps us develop efficient co-developments.

327. The development of our ability to listen increases our chances of achieving efficient co operations.

328. Increasing the strength of our mind augments our possibilities of achieving more efficient co-developments a lot.

329. The capacity of rapid perception helps us a lot to achieve efficient co-developments.

330. Efficient global co operations will contribute in the formation and development of future trust.

331. Humanist global thinking creates great possibilities of development in many areas of activity from many states.

332. Global positive human solidarity helps us achieve more positive efficient human co-developments.

333. Enthusiastic behavior increases our chances of achieving efficient co-developments.

Differences

334. Sometimes something is won by small differences but the first, the winner also has 'n' more advantages than the second.

335. Discipline prevents differences.

336. The ability to solve differences helps us achieve more personal goals.

337. Finding creative solutions that contribute to solving differences helps us achieve more favorable situations.

338. The ability to solve differences helps us achieve much good luck.

339. Finding creative solutions that contribute to solving differences helps us achieve more pleasant surprises.

340. Finding creative solutions that contribute to solving differences helps us achieve more favorable chances.

341. The ability to solve differences helps us achieve more favorable chances.

342. Finding creative solutions that contribute to solving differences helps us achieve more personal goals.

343. The ability to solve differences helps us achieve more records.

344. The ability to solve differences helps us achieve more performances.

345. Finding creative solutions that contribute to solving differences helps us achieve more true friendships.

346. Finding creative solutions that contribute to solving differences helps us achieve more successes.

347. The ability to solve differences helps us achieve more efficient co operations.

348. The ability to solve differences helps us achieve more pleasant surprises.

349. Finding creative solutions that contribute to solving differences helps us achieve more efficient co operations.

350. The ability to solve differences helps us achieve more successes.

351. The ability to solve differences helps us achieve more true friendships.

352. Finding creative solutions that contribute to solving differences helps us achieve more records.

353. Finding creative solutions that contribute to solving differences helps us achieve much good luck.

354. The ability to solve differences helps us achieve more favorable situations.

Diplomatic

355. In order to follow and transform our personal goals into reality, it is necessary to also form, develop, maintain and use our diplomatic behavior.

356. We can form, develop and maintain the state of being ourselves also through the contribution of the formation, development, maintenance and usage of a diplomatic behavior.

357. Problems cannot be solved by the ideas that created them but also through the contribution of the formation, development, maintenance and usage of diplomatic behavior.

358. The solutions to the problems we have or that we want to solve can be found also through the contribution of the formation, development, maintenance and usage of diplomatic behavior.

359. In order to prevent not achieving our personal goals, it is necessary to also form, develop, maintain and use our diplomatic behavior.

360. Our resistance to changing for the better can be overcome also through the contribution of the formation, development, maintenance and usage of diplomatic behavior.

361. We can prevent the falling apart of a happy marriage also through the contribution of the formation, development, maintenance and usage of diplomatic behavior.

362. The obstacles that prevent us from achieving our personal goals can be surpassed also through the contribution of the formation, development, maintenance and usage of diplomatic behavior.

363. The force of our ideas can be augmented also through the contribution of the

formation, development, maintenance and usage of diplomatic behavior.

364. Confidence in ourselves helps us become diplomatic.

365. Continuous self perfection helps us become diplomatic.

366. Release from our self-imposed restrictions can be made also through the contribution of the formation, development, maintenance and usage of diplomatic behavior.

367. Some mistakes can be prevented also through the contribution of the formation, development, maintenance and usage of diplomatic behavior.

368. In order to escape poverty it is necessary to also form, develop, maintain and use diplomatic behavior.

369. We can contribute to the achievement of our greatest accomplishments also through the contribution of the formation, development, maintenance and usage of diplomatic behavior.

370. Obtaining more and greater successes can be achieved also through the contribution of

the formation, development, maintenance, usage of a diplomatic behavior.

Discriminated

371. Discrimination is a great injustice done against those who are discriminated.

372. All over the globe, most of us are discriminated in one way or another once or more times.

373. Sometimes, the discriminated one in a given situation, may discriminate in other circumstances or situation.

374. Young people from all states, which are discriminated in one way or another, need to act with efficiency and continuity to stop discrimination, including through legal actions, petitions, the establishment of non-profit organizations, trade unions, political parties, and other useful institutions in the stopping of all forms of discrimination.

375. When you are discriminated take all necessary measures to end discrimination and avoid the possiblity to get in a position to be discriminated against. You are not

alone. Call institutions that are empowered. Good luck.

376. Life for many people would be more beautiful if they had not been discriminated against.

Discrimination

377. Each of us must prevent discrimination.

378. In the world there are continuous and mass discrimination, although it seems incredible. It is true.

379. Discrimination is one of the biggest causes of poverty for the majority of the people in the world.

380. It is necessary to immediately and continuously join our forces, to be in solidarity to combat all forms of discrimination and to prevent them.

381. Discrimination can be prevented quickly and effectively in the world through solidarity and unity.

382. Among the priorities of the world it is necessary to find the prevention and defeat of discrimination.

383. Discrimination in situations can be defeated, reduced, prevented if it is desired.

384. Discrimination is a great injustice done against those who are discriminated.

385. Discrimination is very harmful to social progress, to all forms of progress.

386. Non-discrimination is a principle that every one of us must act to respect it in all circumstances.

387. Non-discrimination prevents many conflicts.

388. Young people from all states, which are discriminated in one way or another, need to act with efficiency and continuity to stop discrimination, including through legal actions, petitions, the establishment of non-profit organizations, trade unions, political parties, and other useful institutions in the stopping of all forms of discrimination.

389. The long or repeated discrimination of multiple people can sometimes affect health.

390. Discrimination is a very dangerous factor of stress.

391. The state is required to take all measures to prevent discrimination.

392. When you are discriminated take all necessary measures to end discrimination and avoid the possiblity to get in a position to be discriminated against. You are not alone. Call institutions that are empowered. Good luck.

393. Discrimination creates a lot of misfortune in many states.

394. Discrimination has many negative effects, very high in most states.

395. Discrimination very much adversely affects the harmonious development of the personality of many children of the world's states.

396. Unfortunately, discrimination is not prevented and combated as it is necessary in most world states.

397. Discrimination has many negative effects, great ones in most states.

398. Discrimination negatively affects the harmonious development of the personality

of many children, very much, all over the world.

399. Unfortunately, discrimination is not combated and prevented in a necessary way in most world states.

400. States need to support and encourage all those who fight for preventing and stopping discrimination.

401. States must take all the necessary measures for the prevention and stoppage of all forms of discrimination.

402. Discrimination is the cause of many sufferings all over the globe.

403. The discrimination of men towards women, their where it exists, must disappear as soon as possible.

404. The co-development of men and women stop and prevent discriminations.

405. The certainty of respecting the human rights of nondiscrimination is a necessity for each state.

406. The certainty of respecting the rights to non discrimination of people is an obligation for each state.

407. Not respecting the right to nondiscrimination of people by the state is a great abuse.

408. Respecting the right to nondiscrimination of people is mandatory for each person of the planet.

Disputes

409. When respect disappears between spouses in a family, disputes arise, conflicts, arguments, mistrust and ultimately it is very likely in many families for divorce to occur.

410. Abstention is a quality, a behavior that is necessary for both spouses to have because abstention in situations that require the prevention of conflicts, they worsen the negative conflicts, quarrels, misunderstandings, disputes of marriage and sometimes even marriage itself.

411. Disputes that are not constructive are useless and inefficient for both parts or for all the parts involved.

412. Long term thinking can avoid many present disputes that are not constructive.

413. Life is much more beautiful in a marriage when there are no disputes between spouses.

414. The art of solving disputes helps us achieve more records.

415. The art of solving disputes helps us achieve more performances.

416. The art of solving disputes helps us achieve more favorable situations.

417. The art of solving disputes helps us achieve much good luck.

418. The art of solving disputes helps us achieve more favorable chances.

419. The art of solving disputes helps us achieve more personal goals.

420. The art of solving disputes helps us achieve more efficient co operations.

421. The art of solving disputes helps us achieve more true friendships.

422. The art of solving disputes helps us achieve more successes.

423. The art of solving disputes helps us achieve more pleasant surprises.

Disrespect

424. Young people must not remain passive in the face of the disrespect of their rights.

425. Most of those who have not succeeded in achieving a happy marriage up to a certain date, need to form and develop their capacity of fighting against disrespect and discrimination.

426. Each woman has the need not to be disrespected.

Distant

427. We all think about what we will do in the next or more distant days.

428. Our distanced future can be greatly influenced by what we do in the future before that distant future.

429. The more distant the future is the more the factors that will influence it will be more numerous and some more unknown to us.

430. Our distant future can be changed more or less by what we decide now, primarily for our continuing concern of building a certain future of the great changes taking place in society, of the relations, the contacts that we have with various people, of the information that we come in contact with, of the depth and accuracy of the analysis of information we come in contact with, of the creative capacity of our ideas to create new projects, new objectives in the light of our experience, our present , the information we fiind and receive etc.

431. Our orientation towards a very distant future is a creative attitude that helps us a lot to achieve our personal goals.

432. A man with an orientation towards the distant future has greater and more chances to achieve outstanding performances.

433. He who is very distant makes true friends very hard.

434. A man oriented towards the distant future has more and greater chances to become more efficient.

Education

435. States should be especially concerned to achieve a proper education effective from all points of view to respond to real the needs of education of the people and society and to effectively satisfy both their needs.

436. An appropriate efficient education meant to meet the needs of people and society is particularly important for people and for society, but unfortunately, even in 2007, many states do not have a proper effective education to meet the requirements and needs of people and of society concerning education.

437. Advanced education is an engine of our self-achievement.

438. Advanced education contributes a lot to global humanization.

439. An advanced education greatly facilitates the achievement of social relations.

440. An advanced education helps a lot in achieving true love.

441. Education for co-development is a necessity to society.

442. Self- education for co-development is necessary to be a personal goal for each of us.

443. An advanced education contributes greatly to achieving success in life.

444. An advanced education helps us a lot to maintain a happy marriage.

445. Permanent self education helps us a lot to achieve more and greater successes.

446. Permanent self education increases our power continuously.

447. Permanent self education used in solving personal problems increases our trust in ourselves and in our possibilities.

448. Permanent self education helps us become wiser.

449. The education for humanist economy must take the place of the present economical education.

450. Humanist education reduces the insecurity of everyday life very much.

451. Educational needs change continuously and they must be satisfied immediately.

452. Advanced education contributes a lot to self achievement.

453. Advanced education contributes a lot in achieving efficient co-developments.

454. Advanced education contributes a lot to achieving the greater good.

455. Advanced education facilitates the exchange of information.

456. Advanced education contributes and facilitates the creation of true friendships.

457. An advanced education contributes a lot to achieving efficient global co operations.

458. An advanced education contributes greatly to achieving personal goals.

459. Advanced education contributes extensively to achieving the future.

460. Advanced education increases our chances to achieve efficient co operations.

461. Advanced education contributes extensively to achieving more and greater successes.

462. Advanced education contributes sensibly to achieving a positive global future.

463. The meaning of life can be found through the contribution of the formation, development, maintenance and usage of self education.

464. Meanness is also the effect of the absence of our home education.

465. Successes in life can also be achieved thanks to continuous education.

Employment

466. The size of our life is made up of several parts of what it is necessary to know very well in order to achieve each of them. It is not easy but not impossible. First we must know very clearly, concretely that we want to achieve each of them, when, how, we want to achieve them, etc.. Among them we mention privacy that includes our family life, human relations with friends, our intimate life, our feelings and our thoughts, our intimate writings, journals, autobiographies, blogs, web pages etc. To succeed in this life it is necessary to respect, know the rules of success in this private life. Then there is employment, which includes ideas, thoughts, actions, objectives and professional projects. And here in

employment we can succeed only if we respect the rules needed to succeed in our careers. Good behavior is ideal when we can do that to support our private life as much as possible, employment contributes as much as possible to achieve a harmonious private life, with successful private joys, a lot of satisfactions and happiness. If we propose to realize these needs we will establish that we are able to achive personal objectives and performance, great successes, and we will have joys, happiness and satisfactions in life, both in our private and professional one.

Unfortunately, there are still few people who do what they should not do to have failures in both private and professional lives, or in one of them. The most happy and satisfying are called those who made the necessary efforts and who have managed to achieve harmonious, happy privacy, with joys and satisfactions and who have achieved personal goals and projects in employment. From them we can learn many effective models of action, positive behaviors, which will help us achieve our privacy and professionalism.

467. People who are conscientious at work are preferred in employment. So one of the keys to certainly obtain a job is to be conscientious at the workplace. Be aware that you will find a job if you are looking to find it. Do not let yourself beat by obstacles. Good luck. I'm with you.

468. People who return to work immediately and are engaged in employment are maintained. Efficiency at work is a key to obtaining and maintaining employment. Look, learn and practice continuously, day by day to increase your yield continuously so that you have a permanent job and well-paid one. Good luck.

469. The rigorous and disciplined at work have much greater opportunities to obtain and maintain employment. Rigor and discipline at the workplace can be easy if we want to, if we do not have it. Rigor and discipline are two keys to getting a job if you do not have it, or if we have one, they are keys to keeping it. Good luck.

470. Persons who have the quality and ability to realize the tasks accurately and with professionalism have much greater

opportunities to get employment if they do not have jobs and to maintain employment if they have jobs. Therefore it is necessary to continuously develop, day by day our accuracy and professionalism. Good luck.

471. In addition to the knowledge of English or other languages of the country in which we want to ensure work we are more likely to find a job in many situations and to keep our workplace. This is a key addition to enhance our chances to obtain and maintain employment. Learn English or another language that is spoken in the country where you are looking for a job or where you have a job. Good luck.

472. Trade unions must participate constructively, work with the management to streamline employment, to solve problems for working people and companies in order to prevent bankruptcy, unemployment.

473. Trade unions should be more concerned about finding jobs for those who have reduced employment for objective reasons.

474. People who have hopes always have employment.

475. He who is disciplined always has employment.

476. Harmonious global co-development thinking contributes a lot to creating a large number of places to work and to the disappearance of unemployment.

477. Humanist economy will continuously ensure workplaces and useful activities that are positive for all persons on the planet and it will eliminate and prevent unemployment.

Esteemed

478. Inner spiritual beauty makes a woman special, permanently young and a magnet for many men, this makes her much more appreciated, respected and esteemed.

479. Positive thinking makes us do positive deeds, makes us be able to solve our objectives, obtain smaller or greater successes, be appreciated, respected and esteemed, achieve and maintain our happiness, a happy marriage, etc.

480. Polite people are respected, appreciated and esteemed.

481. Communicative people are appreciated, respected, esteemed and rewarded.

482. Magnanimity must be respected, appreciated, esteemed and rewarded.

483. An honest man is appreciated, respected and esteemed by other people.

484. People who help others must be appreciated, respected, esteemed and rewarded.

485. Industrious people must be respected, esteemed and rewarded.

486. People who are forgiving are admired, esteemed, respected and rewarded.

487. A quiet man is very appreciated, esteemed and respected.

488. He who makes correct appreciations is esteemed by people.

489. AGC mediations help us become more esteemed.

Ethical

490. Ethical principles help us a lot in achieving our personal goals.

491. Ethical principles help us a lot in achieving more and greater successes.

492. Ethical principles help us form and develop efficient co-developments.

Existence

493. The existence of abnormal instead of normality has multiple, diversified, negative short-term and long term effects on all people around the world.

494. If two people want to get married and have no common values, the values necessary for the existence and maintenance of a true marriage, they should better not marry, in order to prevent a very painful divorce, a failed marriage.

495. The abnormality's existence in place of normality has multiple diversified, negative short-term and long term effects for all the people around the world.

496. Ego altruistic behavior is a behavior that takes into account both personal interests, of the self and of the other, acting to meet them both for a harmonious coexistence for himself and for the other.

497. The states in which only poverty exists are to blame for the existence of poverty.

498. A realistic man in everything he does achieves his necessary destiny for his existence in life.

499. The richness of existence helps us achieve a more beautiful life.

500. Self security is assured by the existence of just criteria to respect our own value.

501. Skill can assure the existence of a work place.

Freedom

502. Many people are very wrong for dedicating their life only to accumulating riches or financial resources. Some of them risk, in an absurd way, in this pursuit of riches, sometimes, their health, life, freedom, marriage, children, love, etc.. values that are really more valuable than financial and material wealth.

503. Most world members do very little and ineffective things to prevent the disregard of rights and fundamental freedoms.

504. Even in 2007 in the majority of the states of the world so many incredible breaches of fundamental rights and freedoms of humans are made every day, unfortunately.

505. All world members need to take all necessary and effective measures to stop immediately and effectively all disregards of rights and fundamental freedoms.

506. Freedom and democracy have also created more chances and opportunities for personal development.

507. Life is too beautiful to spend part of its freedom in prison to satisfy the desire of luxury.

508. Some journalists risk their work, freedom, health, life for us to offer society and people as much as they can but we do not unfortunately know and do not appreciate them, reward them enough for what they do for us.

509. The world's states have sufficient resources to stop felonies and end the noncompliance with the fundamental rights and freedoms of man, but unfortunately they do not take any measures in this purpose.

510. Most world states work very little and ineffectively to prevent the disregard for human rights and fundamental freedoms.

511. Unfortunately in 2007 in most states of the world there are still every day so many incredible violations of the human rights and fundamental freedoms.

512. All the states in the world need to take all necessary and effective measures to immediately and effectively stop any violation of human rights and fundamental freedoms.

513. Assuring personal freedom is also an individual necessity.

514. Assuring personal freedom must be rewarded.

515. Assuring personal freedom contributes a lot in achieving a happy life.

516. Assuring personal freedom contributes to and helps us become more performing.

517. Freedom in thinking makes us stronger.

518. Assuring the freedom of a person contributes to personal self achievement.

519. Assuring the freedom of a person helps in achieving success in life.

520. Assuring the freedom of a person helps us have more chances to meet favorable situations.

521. The freedom of speech must not be used to broadcast illegal ideas.

522. The freedom of speech must respect human rights.

523. The freedom of speech must respect the law.

524. The freedom of speech is an engine of development in all areas of activity.

525. The freedom of speech contributes a lot in achieving the greater good.

526. The freedom of speech contributes a lot in achieving the desired future for many people.

527. The freedom of speech does not allow broadcasting illegal ideas.

528. The freedom of speech does not allow broadcasting negative ideas that harm people.

529. Assuring personal freedom is necessary to achieve the desired future.

530. Assuring personal freedom ensures the achievement of efficient co operations.

531. Not assuring personal freedom must not be rewarded.

532. Assuring personal freedom ensures the achievement of more and greater successes.

533. Not assuring personal freedom is a great abuse.

534. Not assuring personal freedom makes it very hard to achieve efficient global co operations.

535. Assuring personal freedom contributes a lot to global humanization.

536. Assuring personal freedom prevents many mistakes.

537. Assuring personal freedom contributes a lot to social relations.

538. Assuring personal freedom contributes a lot in preventing many failures.

539. Not assuring personal freedom causes much individual stress.

540. Assuring personal freedom must be promoted.

541. Assuring personal freedom helps us become more efficient.

542. Assuring personal freedom is the right that no one is entitled to dispute.

543. Assuring personal freedom contributes to maintaining efficient co operations.

544. Not assuring personal freedom must not be appreciated.

545. Assuring personal freedom contributes to the achievement of true friendships.

546. Not assuring personal freedom also provokes a mass, collective stress.

547. Not assuring personal freedom makes it very hard to maintain efficient global co operations.

548. Assuring personal freedom must be appreciated.

549. Assuring personal freedom helps achieve outstanding performances.

550. Assuring personal freedom is a social necessity also.

551. Assuring personal freedom must be supported.

552. Assuring personal freedom contributes a lot to achieving a more beautiful life.

553. The safety of personal freedom, unfortunately, even in 2007, is not assured in many states.

554. Not assuring personal freedom must not be supported.

555. Assuring personal freedom contributes a lot to achieving a positive global future.

556. Not assuring personal freedom is a great illegality.

557. Assuring personal freedom contributes a lot to achieving the greater good.

558. Not assuring personal freedom must not be promoted.

559. Assuring personal freedom contributes a lot to achieving personal objectives.

Friendship

560. True friendship can help us pass much easier over the many difficulties of life, and it would not be so if it did not exist.

561. We can resolve some of our problems through the relations of friendship that we have.

562. Solidarity is a factor of many true friendships.

563. Successes often create friendships.

564. Unity is a factor of many lasting friendships.

565. True friendship is a factor of many sustainable co operations.

566. True friendship is a factor of many co-developments.

567. True friendship is a factor of many successes.

568. True friendship is a factor of many records.

569. Understanding is a factor of many lasting friendships.

570. Offenses may destroy many friendships.

571. Uninsipred jokes may destroy many friendships.

572. Through solidarity we can achieve much more true friendships.

573. Some problems we can sometimes solve more quickly only because of relations of friendship.

574. True friendship helps us create other true friends, because it is a visible pattern that makes us more believable before others.

575. True friendship helps us, in need, in dealing with the difficulties that appear in front of us.

576. True friendship gives us more power.

577. I write to be useful and practical. He who writes every day to as many people as possible, helps them in one way or another, but as much as possible to help them achieve personal goals, brave performances, with strong will, with perseverance, to get as much satisfaction,

joy and happiness as they can, to develop a harmonious personality, to be part of as much love for as long as they live, a happy family with happy children, to be hardworking, wise, to have harmony in the family, to have as many relations of friendship and cooperation as they can, to be what makes them better for their family, children and others.

578. Cheerfulness helps us a lot to maintain friendship.

579. Unfairness of any friend in a friendship leads to the disintegration of that friendship.

580. Mutual aid given to each friend in need strengthens friendship.

581. Abnormalities in relations between friends lead to the disintegration of friendship.

582. The quality of friendships is more important than the quantity of friends.

583. Correct relations of friendship make us happy and have positive effects on our health.

584. Common values lead to the achievement and maintenance of friendships.

585. True friendship is formed also due to the common values those who become friends have.

586. True friendship maintains itself and has a long life when the friends who have it have common values.

587. True friendship creates many joys.

588. True friendship makes us not feel lonely.

589. True friendship makes us feel safe.

590. True friendship is an extra card that contributes to achieving other true friendships.

591. True friendship has positive effects on health.

592. True friendship has more positive effects on friends.

593. True friendship makes life more beautiful for those two friends or for that group of friends.

594. People who have the capacity to argue ideas more quickly achieve true friendships.

595. The richness of the heart contributes a lot to achieving true friendships.

596. Working in teams of people with similar values contributes to the formation of many true friendships.

597. Efficient positive human communication contributes a lot to maintaining true friendships.

598. Those who are very conscious have a greater ability to achieve true friendships.

599. Suspicious people hardly realize true friendships.

600. Very sociable people have more and greater chances to achieve more true friendships.

601. Those with the sense of objectivity have greater and more chances to achieve true friendships.

602. Some people with wrong ideas because of some wrong ideas cannot achieve unfortunately any true friendship.

603. True friendship can sometimes make us truly live.

604. True friendship prevents loneliness.

605. True friendship is not achieved by itself.

606. Sometimes our so-called true friends can get us in the biggest troubles possible, can sleep with our wife or with our husband, with our girlfriend or boyfriend, can take away our business, etc. Look around you. Be very careful for the so called true friendship.

607. True friendship is formed and maintained very difficultly and can break in a second. So be very careful. Do not play with it.

608. Friendship and true friendships help us a lot to get over the difficulties and obstacles of life.

609. True friendship becomes stronger and more resistant in time.

610. True friendship is tested in exceptionally difficult situations.

611. True friendship gives us more life, makes us feel truly alive.

612. What true friendship can offer we can only find in it.

613. The majority of people want sincere friendship relations.

614. Loyalty is a quality and value used to maintain true friendship.

615. The lies that two friends tell will break their friendship.

616. In order to maintain a friendship, sincerity is required.

617. Reliability of two friends in a friendship maintains that friendship.

618. Mutual aid given to every friend in need helps maintain the friendship.

619. True friendship is reinforced the more so as to better understand it.

620. The hypocrisy of a friend towards the other leads to the destruction of the friendship.

621. Lies even if they are not very serious, ultimately lead to strained friendship.

622. Even if we have good intentions in a friendship we should not lie to our friend.

Fundamental

623. Most world members do very little and ineffective things to prevent the disregard of rights and fundamental freedoms.

624. Even in 2007 in the majority of the states of the world so many incredible breaches of fundamental rights and freedoms of humans are made every day, unfortunately.

625. All world members need to take all necessary and effective measures to stop immediately and effectively all disregards of rights and fundamental freedoms.

626. Common sense is a fundamental quality which is necessary and required for each of us to have in any situation.

627. Positive thinking is a fundamental engine of progress in all fields.

628. Harmonious global co-development thinking must find the most efficient ideas that are sure an accelerated harmonious global co-development that leads to solving the fundamental needs of mankind.

629. The world's states have sufficient resources to stop felonies and end the noncompliance with the fundamental rights and freedoms of man, but unfortunately they do not take any measures in this purpose.

630. Most world states work very little and ineffectively to prevent the disregard for human rights and fundamental freedoms.

631. Unfortunately in 2007 in most states of the world there are still every day so many incredible violations of the human rights and fundamental freedoms.

632. All the states in the world need to take all necessary and effective measures to immediately and effectively stop any violation of human rights and fundamental freedoms.

Harm

633. Despicable actions we are ultimately harmful to us.

634. Even if the sly actions can help us at a moment, they will harm us eventually.

635. Negative actions can help us at a moment, but they will harm us eventually.

636. Discrimination is very harmful to social progress, to all forms of progress.

637. Haughty behavior is very harmful to us.

638. Hypocrisy is a big flaw that harms us very much in life.

639. Bitterness harms us.

640. The desire to make one's way in life by any means is very harmful to anyone.

641. Anger harms us always.

642. Sorrows that are often do us much harm.

643. We do harm to our marriage if we bore with naggings the one that we married.

644. We are always harmed by sorrows.

645. We must never do something that harms us.

646. The one who is quick in anger does himself much harm.

647. Those who will consider wise advice will grow a more harmonious personality.

648. Totalitarianism is harmful to people.

649. The harmonious development of our personality is a source of our happiness.

650. The harmonious development of our personality is a factor of our successes.

651. One of the objectives of our life should be the harmonious development of our personality.

652. Conceit is very harmful to us.

653. Positive thinking prevents much harm.

654. We should never allow ourselves to be tempted by anything that harms us or harms others.

655. Hypocrisy is a defect that harms people very much.

656. Indecision can sometimes harm us very much.

657. Considering a false value as a value is enormously harmful.

658. Intrigues are so very harmful both to schemers and to the ones affected by intrigue.

659. Harmony is a factor of many successes.

660. Harmony is good for our health.

661. Arrogance can sometimes cause us much harm.

662. Shrewish behavior harms us.

663. Shrewish behavior prevents harmony in a family.

664. He who is greedy can sometimes cause much harm to himself.

665. He who is brutal can sometimes cause much harm to himself.

666. When we offend we can do much harm.

667. When we offend we can do ourselves much harm.

668. He who is false in behaviour creates his own harm.

669. A charming man attracts the attention of many women.

670. A charming woman seduces many men.

671. Extening the duration in which we grieve for something will harm us very much sometimes.

672. A charming woman draws the attention of many men.

673. Riotousness sometimes harm us very much.

674. Excess is harmful to us.

675. The state of discouragement does us no good, it can consume us inside, it can harm us over a longer period of time.

676. We must always seek and find solutions so that troubles do not harm our health.

677. Many of us harm our own health.

678. Pride is harmful to us.

679. Not doing something on time can harm us very much sometimes.

680. Brutality harm us very much.

681. Sadness can still harm very much our health.

682. Intermittent but repeated sadness can sometimes harm our health very much.

683. Immorality is enormously harmful to society.

684. It is necessary in life to do only things that do not harm us or others.

685. He who is a bastard harms himself with his blackness.

686. Repeated irritations can even harm our health.

687. We do not have the right to joke with something that harms or may harm others.

688. Before joking it is necessary to think whether it is good to joke or not, if the joke can harm us or can harm another or others.

689. Not thinking is very harmful in many situations.

690. Prejudices sometimes harm us enormously. That is why it is necessary to discover all the prejudices and not let them lead us in certain situations.

691. Repeated failures can sometimes harm our health very much.

692. Unfortunately, most people in most cases use only short-term thinking which mostly harms those around them.

693. Divorces are extremely harmful to both men and women but more harmful to children.

694. Most of the time it is too easy to divorce, for both men and women, not thinking enough about their children, about the negative

effects of divorce on children and their spouses and harming themselves.

695. By allowing what is bad can sometimes cause us much harm.

696. Tact within the family contributes a lot to maintaining harmony and understanding.

697. Corruption is so generalized in the world and so harmful that it constitutes a global danger of humanity, the greatest and the most dangerous and with negative effects that it creates for society.

698. The loss of family ties, enormous harms the one who lost them, sometimes having some very large negative effects for that person, unbalancing his life.

699. Loneliness is very harmful to those who are lonely, it has more negative effects on the lonely person.

700. A husband's love for the woman is also manifested by the harmonious and continuous communication with his wife.

701. Both the wife and husband should not provoke jealousy to each other because this can harm them enormously much in certain

situations, and even lead to divorce, to arguments and continuous conflict, unbearable tension which could lead to divorce.

702. Such people can go from failure to failure and make their own life to be hell, as they are sometimes led by their desires and their behavior harms anyone who meets these sometimes subjective desires. This harmful behavior primarily hurts ourselves and it is necessary to prevent it not to satisfy our subjective desires that harm us more or less.

703. The continuous return of any harmful behavior for us is one of the factors that make us happy a lot of times.

704. At the moment on the Internet and in the books written so far, we can find sufficient information to certainly help us build our own happiness in harmonious family relationships and with other people. It is necessary to establish the present and future that through their achievement make us happy and act effectively and with continuous dedication to attain them.

705. Spouses need and must be respectful to one another to maintain harmony, understanding and happiness in the family.

706. In a family, its members may not joke with what could negatively affect the harmony, understanding and happiness of the family and sometimes with what could lead to divorce.

707. For a family to prevent divorce, it is necessary to do everything they can to preserve the marriage, harmony, understanding, etc..

708. Spouses need to comply with those rules in the family that make them have good relations and harmony in the family.

709. Both spouses need to continuously do everything that depends on them to have harmony between them. Harmony is a part of their happiness.

710. The brutality between spouses enormously harms the marriage.

Hatred

711. Hatred is extremely dangerous.

712. Hatred many times creates arguments.

713. Hatred is a primitive behavior.

714. Hatred creates psychical discomfort.

715. Hatred makes relationships between people worse.

716. Hatred is born even between brothers.

717. It is necessary that we always prevent hatred.

718. He who hates can escape hatred.

719. Hatred can create hatred many times.

720. Hatred causes arguments between those who hate each other.

721. Hatred is very harmful to the one who hates.

Himself

722. He who hates harms himself.

723. A man sure of himself has great chances to achieve a more beautiful life.

724. A man who knows how to protect himself must know how to choose his friends.

725. Man's need to achieve himself has contributed greatly to achieving the greater good.

726. He who says unconsidered words many times harms himself.

727. He who says unconsidered words can many times harm others too, not only himself.

728. He who is sure of himself has more chances to face stressing situations.

729. A reliable man has the potential to help himself achieve a happy life.

730. A man sure of himself has great chances of achieving efficient co-developments.

731. A man who knows how to protect himself has thrust in himself.

732. A man sure of himself has much more and greater chances to meet more favorable situations.

733. A man who knows how to protect himself permanently takes preventive measures.

734. A conscious man changes his life for the better by himself.

735. A man sure of himself more easily achieves true friendships.

736. A man who knows how to protect himself can prevent many mistakes.

737. A man's need to achieve himself has continuously contributed to increasing the efficiency of human actions.

738. A man with a good imagination of himself has a greater confidence in himself.

739. An open man has much more chances to achieve a happy life for himself.

740. A man sure of himself has great possibilities to achieve outstanding performances.

741. A man with tactical values accomplishes himself in life.

742. A man who knows how to protect himself is resistant to stress.

743. A man sure of himself most of the times knows how to efficiently manage his time.

744. A man who knows how to protect himself continuously makes exchanges of ideas.

745. The optimistic man has more chances to surpass himself.

746. A vigilant man has more chances to perfect himself.

747. A vigilant man has more chances to surpass himself.

Honesty

748. Honesty is a quality that prevents many misdoings.

749. Honesty is a quality that makes people happy.

750. Those who do not properly appreciate honesty are not humane.

751. What is built on honesty is very solid.

752. Honesty brings us luck.

753. An honest woman through her honesty and her qualities maintains a happy marriage.

754. Honesty demands honesty.

755. True friendships rely on honesty.

Human

756. An official who does not respect human rights should be dismissed immediately.

757. Many of the serious human errors could have been prevented.

758. Many of the serious human errors can be prevented.

759. Human experience accumulated so far, a part of it stored in books, on the Internet, etc.. gives and creates large opportunities for us to have a happy life if we study and depict it.

760. Hospitality strengthens our human relations.

761. It is necessary at all times to develop our human qualities.

762. Human qualities contribute the most to human success.

763. Human skills contribute greatly to human successes.

764. Humanism is a quality required for each man in order to create a more humane society.

765. Humanism contributes to avoiding more trouble.

766. Humanism contributes to avoiding many misdoings.

767. Judges which during their professional activity have committed breaches of human rights must necessarily give their resignation themselves.

768. The effects of human actions have an increasing influence on the environment. This makes us think on a global scale, long-term and scientific before acting and makes us perform more profound studies, of impact, regarding our actions, to prevent the implementation of actions that have negative, inadmissible effects on the environment, society and people.

769. Young people from all of the world's states should not be negligent, careless, passive, inactive, non-participative in taking decisions that concern them, their present and future, but to take part in decision-making in local councils, central parliaments, governments and other state and non-state institutions, and use all their capacities, abilities, skills, attitudes, knowledge, energy, commitment

and desire to assert and achieve great deeds, to create a more humane, more righteous, more happy, with less trouble world.

770. For a marriage to survive in the long term it is necessary for spouses to do everything humanly possible and normal to maintain and sustain mutual love.

771. The more positive and humane deeds we accomplish, the more we increase our chances of being happy.

772. For the sake of ourselves and of others, of human society, it is necessary and mandatory to appreciate and respect positive thinking.

773. For our sake and that of others, of human society, it is necessary and required to appreciate, promote and apply positive ideas.

774. For our sake and that of others, of human society, it is necessary and required to appreciate, promote and apply positive programs and projects.

775. For our sake and that of others, of human society, it is necessary to appreciate, reward and promote positive actions.

776. In life it is necessary to self-impose voluntarily and not obliged by anyone our personal humane goals.

777. The science of raising children would increase the quality of human beings.

778. Human qualities contribute the most to human successes.

779. Human qualities make a lot of people happy.

780. Human decadence should never be supported.

781. Dehumanization is very dangerous to society.

782. We muat always prevent the causes that lead to dehumanization.

783. Dehumanization must be prevented.

784. Societies that do not prevent dehumanization situations are inhumane societies.

785. The dehumanized man can cause very big human tragedies.

786. Most human errors can be prevented.

787. It is necessary to develop the science of preventing human errors.

788. The science of preventing human errors should include knowledge of prevention of human errors for each field of activity and every human action.

789. The science of preventing human errors would accelerate progress in every field of activity.

790. The science of preventing human errors would prevent billions of human mistakes.

791. The science of preventing human errors would lead to a more efficient management of resources that are available to man.

792. The science of preventing human errors should accelerate improvements in the quality of life of people around the globe.

793. The development and practical application of the science of preventing human errors would have positive effects for all people in

the world, incalculable, many, very deep, very different, incredible effects.

794. A society that has street children, street people, etc. is an inhumane society.

795. Human resources are enormous, incalculable, a fact which can make people's lives achieve a much better quality.

796. Due to enormous progress of human knowledge that is continuously growing daily, daily, the number of new opportunities to create a better quality of life is getting better.

797. Unfortunately, enormously many people are not concerned to find and use human knowledge that can help enormously hard to achieve a much better quality of life.

798. Human knowledge should be used effectively, organized, planned, impersonal, humanist for the good of our people and, in an incredibly short time, the quality of life of billions of people would grow incredibly much.

799. Most people today do not know how to use all of human knowledge that they could use to make their life much better.

800. Each of us can come, by using the Internet, to get to know human knowledge that can help us greatly in increasing the quality of our life.

801. Unfortunately, many times no protection by the society of those who need it has enormously negative effects and multiple ones that are irreversible on them, sometimes resulting in suicides, deaths, self-mutilations, killings, physical and psychological damage, some irreversible, crimes with many years of conviction, inhuman life under the open sky, on the streets, in suers, etc.

802. It is inadmissible that in the 21st century human tragedies exist in such an incredibly high number.

Humanity

803. A great capacity of assuming the necessary risks for achieving personal goals helps us maintain our humanity.

804. A great capacity of being friendly helps us maintain our humanity.

805. A great capacity of achieving what was proposed helps us maintain our humanity.

806. A great capacity of forming a positive own lifestyle helps us maintain our humanity.

807. A great capacity of assuming the necessary risks for success helps us maintain our humanity.

808. A great capacity of using attitudes helps us maintain our humanity.

809. A great capacity of continuously overcoming boundaries helps us maintain our humanity.

810. A great capacity of using a value system helps us maintain our humanity.

811. A great capacity of positively influencing people helps us maintain our humanity.

812. A great capacity of being convincing helps us maintain our humanity.

813. A great capacity of accomplishing strategies of applying thinking on a big scale helps us maintain our humanity.

814. A great capacity of self-surpassing helps us maintain our humanity.

815. The dream to the grand helps us maintain our humanity.

816. A great capacity of using each personal mistake to achieve successes helps us maintain our humanity.

817. A great capacity of remaining involved in the same area with even greater objectives helps us maintain our humanity.

818. A great capacity of rapid instruction helps us maintain our humanity.

819. A great capacity of facing one's own life helps us maintain our humanity.

820. A great capacity of establishing great personal goals helps us maintain our humanity.

821. A great capacity of assuming the necessary risks for achieving great successes helps us maintain our humanity.

822. A great capacity of using qualities helps us maintain our humanity.

823. A great capacity of maintaining a positive efficient own lifestyle helps us maintain our humanity.

824. A great capacity of being popular helps us maintain our humanity.

825. A great capacity of using available ideas helps us maintain our humanity.

826. A great capacity of creating one's own safety helps us maintain our humanity.

827. A great capacity of using each failure to achieve successes helps us maintain our humanity.

828. A great capacity of doing what is best helps us maintain our humanity.

829. A great capacity of increasing creativity helps us maintain our humanity.

830. A great capacity of adopting visions helps us maintain our humanity.

Ignorance

831. Ignorance is a cause of much unhappiness.

832. Ignorance is a cause of many misunderstandings.

833. Ignorance can be prevented if we have will.

834. Our ignorance is the cause of many of our troubles.

835. Ignorance, very often, makes us skeptical.

836. Ignorance produces a lot of dark evil.

837. Ignorance produces darkness and envy.

838. Ignorance is directly or indirectly the cause of most crimes.

839. The uneducated man is harmful because of a lot of ignorance.

840. Ignorance is a factor of many misfortunes.

841. Aggression is a result of ignorance.

842. Sometimes ignorance makes our life very complicated.

843. Meanness is a result of ignorance.

844. Ignorance produces much evil.

845. Ignorance also produces envy.

846. Ignorance is the cause of many arguments.

847. Ignorance is the cause of many mistakes.

848. Ignorance is the cause of many divorces.

849. Ignorance is a cause of pessimism.

850. Ignorance is the cause of many failures.

Illegal

851. We can prevent more failures if we analyze our actions, their positive and negative effects, so that we and others achieve and avoid actions with negative, risky, illegal effects.

852. To accuse someone intentionally in an illegal way is a crime.

853. He who is accused in bad faith, illegally, has long suffered unjustly.

854. The honest man refuses to make illegal business.

855. Unfortunately, society is not concerned enough, does not take the necessary measures to prevent the causes that lead certain people in a position where they need social protection and ensure the needed and obligatory human protection for people who need it.

856. In fact, through this inhuman, ineffective, irresponsible, illegal, selfish, abusive, etc. behavior, society, unfortunately, has a great contribution to the achievement of many crimes committed by people who needed human protection and were not given any.

857. Society, among its priorities should also have the following priorities:

858. 1) To create the necessary institutions and to take the necessary measures to prevent with maximum effectiveness, efficiency and safety all the causes leading to the creation of situations where some people need human protection;

859. 2) To create the institution: The Authority of Human Protection (1) to verify the state's institutions, individuals and private or illegal entities if they prevent the creation of the causes leading to some situations where people need human protection (2) and if they provide the human protection necessary for people who need this protection.

860. Any act of aggression against a family member by another family member is illegal and can be punished by the law.

861. It is illegal to try to make others responsible for your own failures.

862. Artfulness helps us to discover ruses, but after the discovery they could be extremely harmful depending on the seriousness of the illegal actions made and the size of their negative effects.

863. It is necessary and we must never forget what tempts us harms us or others illegally.

864. It is easier to prevent illegal actions than to fix the negative effects.

865. It is best not to not think about illegal actions, not to commit them.

866. So as not to commit illegal acts intentionally we must prevent them or at least think about them.

867. Those who have argued that their illegalities can not be discovered are terribly wrong.

868. Some lawyers, many believe it, have participated actively and passively to the

achievement of many injustices, illegalities of their clients, worldwide, in almost all the countries of the world.

869. Unfortunately in many states there still is no justice, there is injustice, given the number of inadmissible irregularities, decisions handed down virtually illegally and that exceed those laws in some states.

870. A judge must give a lesser punishment because it is wrong to give a greater punishment illegally.

871. A judge makes a lesser mistake if he gives a smaller sentence than to abuse and be wrong so as to give an illegally bigger punishment.

872. A judge makes a grater mistake if he gives a bigger sentence to a person who does not have sufficient evidence to convince him that the defendant is guilty 100% than punishes him with X years in prison in an abusive, illegal way.

873. Illegal actions lead us to prison. Warning. You can easily go to prison. Read the Criminal Code.

874.   Illegal actions can never be perfectly covered so as not to be discovered. So attention, you would better not do it.

875.   Illegal actions can destroy mature, true love. Is it worth it? No. So be careful.

876.   Think of yourselves when you do something legal or illegal even if the guilty one can go to prison. You had better pay extra attention; it does not require great efforts and is not worth doing many years in prisons.

877.   Discovered illegal actions create very large damages often to those who have done them. So, pay much attention, better think it over a hundred times than face the negative effects of an illegal action that you rushed to make. What do you think?

878.   Is it worth not doing illegal acts.

879.   The favorable effects of illegal actions will often be scattered with money for lawyers, for roads and visits to prisons, health degradation in prison, etc..

880.   Illegal actions can destroy happy marriages. So pay much attention.

881. It is best neither to think of illegal actions, nor do them.

882. We can not do illegal actions on purpose by preventing them, or at least by not thinking of them.

883. Those who have the idea that their illegalities not being discovered are very much mistaken.

884. Unfortunately, a number of lawyers should be behind bars because of the many crimes they have done, because of the misfortunes and damage they have done, because of illegal behaviors in their relationship with their clients.

885. Some lawyers, incredibly many of them, have participated actively and positively to the achievement of many injustices, illegalities of their clients worldwide, nearly all over the world.

886. A judge must give a smaller sentence than be mistaken and give a greater sentence illegally.

Immoral

887. Immorality is enormously harmful to society.

888. It is immoral for a man to seduce the girlfriend of his best friend.

889. Lust is immoral.

890. Immorality makes the immoral ones be rejected by others.

891. Immorality undermines the very immoral one.

892. Immorality is a factor of many failures.

893. Immorality is a question of many misfortunes.

894. He who is immoral is not credible in many situations.

Impersonal

895. Human knowledge should be used effectively, organized, planned, impersonal, humanist for the good of our people and, in an incredibly short time, the quality of life of billions of people would grow incredibly much.

896. Our happiness depends a lot also on the formation, development, maintenance and usage of impersonal behavior.

897. We can contribute to the achievement of our greatest accomplishments also through the contribution of the formation, development, maintenance and usage of impersonal behavior.

898. Problems cannot be solved by the ideas that created them but also through the contribution of the formation, development, maintenance and usage of impersonal behavior.

899. Obtaining more and greater successes can be achieved also through the contribution of the formation, development, maintenance, usage of an impersonal behavior.

900. In order to escape poverty it is necessary to also form, develop, maintain and use impersonal behavior.

901. The obstacles that prevent us from achieving our personal goals can be surpassed also through the contribution of the formation, development, maintenance and usage of impersonal behavior.

902. Some mistakes can be prevented also through the contribution of the formation,

development, maintenance and usage of impersonal behavior.

903. Hopes can be created also through the contribution of the formation, development, maintenance and usage of impersonal behavior.

904. We can form, develop and maintain the state of being ourselves also through the contribution of the formation, development, maintenance and usage of an impersonal behavior.

905. Our resistance to changing for the better can be overcome also through the contribution of the formation, development, maintenance and usage of impersonal behavior.

906. Rather than lamenting that we do not have successes it is more useful to also form, develop, maintain and use impersonal behavior.

907. The force of our ideas can be augmented also through the contribution of the formation, development, maintenance and usage of impersonal behavior.

908. We can prevent the falling apart of a happy marriage also through the contribution of the formation, development, maintenance and usage of impersonal behavior.

909. We can prevent some failures also through the contribution of the formation, development, maintenance and usage of impersonal behavior.

910. Acting efficiently helps us become impersonal.

911. The necessary qualities in achieving personal goals can be formed, developed, maintained and used also through the contribution of the formation, development, maintenance and usage of impersonal behavior.

912. Aspiring towards a more meaningful life can also be achieved through the formation, development, maintenance and usage of impersonal behavior.

913. Continuous self-motivation helps us become impersonal.

914. We can become stronger and we can not allow ourselves to be influenced by the

world also through the contribution of the formation, development, maintenance and usage of impersonal behavior.

915. We can overcome the difficulties that we must overcome also through the help of the formation, development, maintenance and usage of impersonal behavior.

916. Stress can be prevented also through the formation, development, maintenance and usage of impersonal behavior.

Importance

917. The attention given to justice by the society is enormously small as compared to the importance of justice to the society and people.

918. Very often, we deal with many issues of lesser importance, of lesser urgency instead of more important and urgent problems.

919. Only by making a correct hierarchy, all the time, of our personal goals, according to importance and urgency, we can achieve more personal goals.

920. The science of raising children needs to become the object and subject of study in schools, universities, due to its importance.

921. Unfortunately, today's creative thinking and its development is allocated a time inversely proportional to the importance and usefulness of them for every man and society.

922. Spiritual self-development is necessary, it is useful and it should become mandatory for each person as a personal goal due to the importance, necessity, utility, the requirement for spiritual development of each person of this planet, of countries and of all mankind. Spiritual self-development is a major highly efficient form of the development of our spiritual life.

923. Spiritual self-development is necessary and required due to its importance for each human to become a personal goal for as long as we live.

924. Each of us has had one or more bigger or smaller failures. It's good not to have any failures or as few failures as possible. Some or more failures could harm us very much. Those who were careful did not achieve

failure or failures and have made smaller, fewer ones. Prevision helps us prevent many failures. The more experienced in previsioning we are, the greater ability we have to provide, as we have more knowledge necessary to achieve previsions etc.. the more we can make accurate previsions, prevent many mistakes, failures, trouble, accidents, conflicts, arguments, unsuccessful actions, etc. In our personal and professional life, it is necessary to continuously develop and to have that personal goal to develop to a maximum capacity the prevision in private life, the ability to use previsions. We can continuously increase the capacity of our prevision very much, as we live if we have personal objectives, as we expand our ability to prevision and whether we act to continuously and effectively achieve this objective. Those who aimed at personal living as to develop the capacity of prevision continuously and concretely act with dedication to achieve their capacity to make a prevision which will help them achieve one or more very big successes, they will succeed to prevent many failures, troubles, etc., they will be able to achieve much in life, to have many happy, satisfying moments and so much happiness. The more we have a capacity of more than prevision, a more accurate, more efficient one, the more valuable we are for having this treasure. This treasure we can continuously increase greatly. The capacity of prevision generally contains more capacities of prevision in some actions, behaviors in the achievement of personal objectives, private, professional, specific ones, etc. It is necessary to develop those capabilities specific to prediction that we need. Knowledge, experience, qualifications, skills, etc., in a specific prevision capacity can be used to a greater or lesser degree in other capacities specific to prevision. The capacities of prevision are very necessary and very useful to us but unfortunately very few people have personal goals in life to continuously develop the specific performance of prevision. Due to the special importance of the capacity of prevision it is necessary and required to create and develop the science of the development of the capacity of prevision, because having this science we would have it by applying enormous positive effects on countless people that should develop and apply it indirectly on other people. The state would accelerate progress in many fields, would accelerate the reduction of illiteracy, poverty, illness, divorces out of arguments and conflict, accidents, what harms humans, animals, the environment, etc.. It would lead to solving many personal and state targets, it would create enormously many joys, much satisfaction and happiness. It would lead to the situation that most people no longer live at the whim of chance, with no personal, professional security, etc.. but on the contrary they would lead to more people having them as an objective and as they continue to live, they would develop the personal capacities necessary for their prevision and apply them every day, both in the establishment of private personal or professional life, it would be something concrete that will help them achieve more harmonious lives to achieve what they want and need for their families.

925. There is the capacity of prevision in specific persons, specific societies, specific legal entities, nonprofit organizations, companies, banks, groups, collectivities, international and intergovernmental organizations. Both individuals and legal entities, must not live

from hand to mouth, must act firmly, must study and evaluate the effects of positive and negative actions, decisions, etc. their objectives are also necessary to be: 1) to aim at continuing to develop their capacities of specific prediction that they need, 2) to apply, continuous use in any action, situation-specific prediction capabilities necessary and useful efforts, energy consumption and costs for the development and capacity of specific prevision that they need.

926.   Failures can happen in each of our actions or less often. Our failures can be created by factors and actions sometimes difficult to identify and prevent. However there are actions where we can know all the factors that can create failures. Knowing the factors that create failures in actions, we can take the necessary measures to prevent them by reaching in some cases to zero failures, as they have succeeded in situations in a long time, in many states, especially people in the most developed countries of the world. How to develop more this science with the more than we can know more of the factors that could cause failures in certain situations to certain actions. Scientific knowledge can

contribute greatly to preventing many failures in many actions. At present people do not use scientific knowledge, the human experience gained in books, studies, on the Internet, although they have committed enormously many failures, mistakes, although they could prevent many huge mistakes, failures if they would use efficient, organized, timely human experience and knowledge from books, the Internet when they would need it. Countries should take immediate measures and be more interested in people and use them when they need knowledge and human experience that can reach and can be used. Human knowledge is growing and increases daily awfully much, and human experience which can create the situation so that we can prevent every day more even more mistakes and failures with positive effects on our high society, to accelerate progress in many areas.

927. Where we have failures we should never discourage and lose our wits, our balance inside, our optimism, morale or to start to grieve. If we do this, it would solve absolutely no problem, but on the contrary, it would stress us illogically, abnormally

without any positive effects. Those who have achieved many successes knew how to cope with failure, learning from failures, to reduce the negative effects of failures. Many failures rather than strengthening us, they weaken us, they should give us power instead of imobilizing us and mobilize us instead of making them harder to give motivation, instead of multiple negative effects they should have have multiple positive effects.

928. However, I disagree and do not consider as logical, positive or constructive the popular saying: „Man learns from mistakes". Man, on the contrary should learn only from his successes and from those who have achieved successes and gained, by imitating those positive behaviors, which have effectively contributed to success. In addition man can learn enormously not to have failures, or make mistakes from the knowledge and positive experience of mankind stored in books, media, on the Internet and the experience of people who have huge experience and knowledge. The more we can prevent more failures, mistakes, the more we can prevent more and more different negative effects.

929. It would be necessary and useful the development of a science to prevent human errors because it would prevent a large number of human errors and failures if people study and apply it as much and in as many actions as they can. This knowledge could and should be studied in colleges and universities and other educational forms. In every area of activity for each action type, it could identify factors that create human mistakes and failures and then it could identify solutions and measures to be taken to prevent mistakes and failures.

930. Efforts and expenses that will be done by creating, developing, learning and applicating the science to prevent human errors will not be much lower than the positive effects of their prevention of a very large number of mistakes and failures and their multiple, diverse and very large negative effects. Financial investment, energy, time, etc.. in these activities related to the prevention of human errors and failures would be very effective and necessary and useful for both countries and for people in particular. Each of us in a greater or lesser way can participate in the

creation, development and application of the science to prevent human errors.

931. The world does not provide the conditions necessary and mandatory for the activities necessary to achieve a performance in raising children and its importance.

932. Husbands should never forget the importance of sex in maintaining a happy marriage.

933. The objective of personal planning for our actions continuously, day by day, for as long as we live, contributes greatly to achieving our other goals. It deserves to get our attention because of its importance. Good luck.

934. The personal goal of effectively organizing our actions continuously, day by day, for as long as we live, contributes greatly to achieving other of our personal objectives. It deserves to receive the necessary attention, because of its importance. Good luck.

935. Increasing the efficiency of justice should be one of the main objectives of each state, because it is of little importance in many states.

936. The work of journalists should be more supported by the society, the state and the people, because of its special importance to the good of the people.

937. The economy of knowledge will be an integral part of maximum importance in humanist economy.

938. Unfortunately enormously many people do not to give the importance, the attention or the time needed for a true marriage.

939. The force of our words can be increased through the importance of the message we transmit.

940. The force of our words can be augmented through the importance of the message we transmit.

Inadmissible

941. The effects of human actions have an increasing influence on the environment. This makes us think on a global scale, long-term and scientific before acting and makes us perform more profound studies, of impact, regarding our actions, to prevent the implementation of actions that have

negative, inadmissible effects on the environment, society and people.

942. It is inadmissible that in the 21st century human tragedies exist in such an incredibly high number.

943. Unfortunately in many states there still is no justice, there is injustice, given the number of inadmissible irregularities, decisions handed down virtually illegally and that exceed those laws in some states.

944. Any act of aggression of one member by another family member is inadmissible and can not be justified.

Incorrect

945. Our happiness is sometimes influenced by our correct or incorrect perception of our situation.

946. Envy is an incorrect behavior that damages us, and sometimes it can cause us enormously much damage.

947. Enmities are incorrect behaviors that damage, sometimes, both us, as well as those who are our enemies.

948. Incorrect behavior of the husband towards his wife leads to decreased confidence of the wife in the husband.

949. Incorrect behavior of the husband towards the wife leads to decreased confidence in her husband.

950. Anger is an incorrect behavior with multiple negative effects.

951. Constructive thinking makes us have zero tolerance towards incorrect thinking.

952. When we see life in an incorrect way it harms us a lot.

953. Those who see life in an incorrect way have a lot to suffer in life.

954. Our way of seeing love relations can be correct or incorrect.

955. Our way of seeing love relations, if it is incorrect stops the achievement of true love.

956. Our way of seeing family relations can be correct or incorrect.

Inhuman

957. Societies that do not prevent dehumanization situations are inhumane societies.

958. A society that has street children, street people, etc. is an inhumane society.

959. Unfortunately, many times no protection by the society of those who need it has enormously negative effects and multiple ones that are irreversible on them, sometimes resulting in suicides, deaths, self-mutilations, killings, physical and psychological damage, some irreversible, crimes with many years of conviction, inhuman life under the open sky, on the streets, in suers, etc.

960. Unfortunately, society is not concerned enough, does not take the necessary measures to prevent the causes that lead certain people in a position where they need social protection and ensure the needed and obligatory human protection for people who need it.

961. In fact, through this inhuman, ineffective, irresponsible, illegal, selfish, abusive, etc.

behavior, society, unfortunately, has a great contribution to the achievement of many crimes committed by people who needed human protection and were not given any.

962. The systems, the formal measures of the state made to solve human problems, the judicial system with certain behaviors typical to slave-owning, feudal, totalitarian, communist, inhuman, against man etc. societies. Many times in many situations people can decay morally, degrade mentally and physically, degrade their health, be an expert in crimes.

963. If we somehow have inhumane behavior it is necessary to change immediately to human behavior.

964. Inhumane behaviors are primitive behaviors.

965. If we somehow have any inhumane behavior it is necessary to change to human behavior immediately.

966. People who have been in prison rightfully or wrongly, if, after they are released from inhuman prisons they succeed to have even

more successes, some of which are unbelievable, they must be respected.

967. People who have been in prison rightfully or wrongly, if, after their coming out of inhuman prisons, have achieved more and greater incredible successes, have more chances to achieve their desired future.

968. People who have been in prison rightfully or wrongly, if, after being released from inhuman prisons have gathered many and great successes, they have more chances to prevent most of their future mistakes.

Injustice

969. Discrimination is a great injustice done against those who are discriminated.

970. He who makes an injustice most often commits a crime.

971. Injustice is also an abuse.

972. Any injustice that could be done to us should not discourage us.

973. The judge who committed an injustice is necessary and required to answer criminaly, civily, financialy, for that injustice.

974. If we are right, any injustice we would do during the process must not, under any circumstances leave us defeated.

975. If we are right, and have injustice in the law suits, it must give us greater powers to overcome injustice for us and to finally win justice.

976. A judge who made a single injustice, has no moral right to judge. What to say to those who do daily tens of deeds of injustice, or annually thousands of deeds of injustice?

977. We should never be careless about injustice.

978. It is necessary and imperative that all countries take the necessary measures, continuously, day by day, to prevent any possible injustice.

979. Any injustice should be removed in the shortest time.

980. The one who has made an injustice is necessary to respond criminally and civilly for the injustice done.

981. Some lawyers, many believe it, have participated actively and passively to the achievement of many injustices, illegalities

of their clients, worldwide, in almost all the countries of the world.

982. Unfortunately in many states there still is no justice, there is injustice, given the number of inadmissible irregularities, decisions handed down virtually illegally and that exceed those laws in some states.

983. Some lawyers, incredibly many of them, have participated actively and positively to the achievement of many injustices, illegalities of their clients worldwide, nearly all over the world.

984. Unfortunately, in many states there is still no justice, there is injustice, because the number of intolerable offenses, unlawful decisions pronounced which virtually surpass those just ones in some states.

985. Illegal actions of justice create many damages, misfortunes, sufferings and injustices.

986. Violence can sometimes be generated by many social injustices.

987. In order to prevent violence in society the state needs to prevent injustice,

discrimination and everything that is harmful to people.

988. I can feel a strong psychical discomfort when I see injustices done to people.

989. A great capacity of using each injustice received in order to achieve successes helps us become more loving.

990. A great capacity of using each injustice received in order to achieve successes helps us become enthusiastic.

991. A great capacity of using each injustice received in order to achieve successes helps us maintain our way of being cautious.

992. A great capacity of using each injustice received in order to achieve successes helps us become efficient.

993. A great capacity of using each injustice received in order to achieve successes helps us become happier.

994. A great capacity of using each injustice received in order to achieve successes helps us achieve more efficient co operations.

995. A great capacity of using each injustice received in order to achieve successes must be formed.

Inter-human

996. The Internet helps us develop the necessary skills and training for inter-humane relations.

997. The Internet helps us develop the necessary training skills for inter-human relations.

998. A sociable and open person more easily achieves inter-human relations.

999. When we have problems in inter-human relations we must find the causes of problems.

1000. Argumentative talks harm inter-human relations.

1001. The exteriorization of our discontents in inter-human relations contributes to maintaining those relations.

1002. When people reveal their feelings mutually they contribute a lot to maintaining inter-human relations.

1003. Optimism does a lot of good to inter-human relations.

1004. Arrogance is very harmful to inter-human relationships.

1005. Contentious behavior is very harmful to inter-human relations.

1006. Contentious behavior must be eliminated in inter-human relations.

1007. AGC mediations reflect on what should be inter-human relations.

1008. Inter-human communication must be appreciated.

1009. Inter-human communication must be rewarded.

1010. Inter-human communication must be supported.

1011. Inter-human communication must be encouraged.

1012. Inter-human communication must be a model.

1013. Inter-human communication must be imitated.

1014. Inter-human communication must be maintained.

1015. Inter-human communication must be used.

International

1016. All employees of international organizations and states, which act during the performance of their duties with irresponsibility should be dismissed immediately and effective measures to recover the damage created by their irresponsible actions should be taken.

1017. All employees of states and international institutions must be operational and efficient in their actions because their actions are very necessary, and if not, it is necessary and required to resign and be replaced with others who have the necessary efficiency and operativity.

1018. States and international organizations have the right and obligation to create themselves conditions so that citizens can be able to handle jobs in which they are most effective and operational and it must reward them properly, in order to keep them in those positions.

1019. Each of us has had one or more bigger or smaller failures. It's good not to have any

149

failures or as few failures as possible. Some or more failures could harm us very much. Those who were careful did not achieve failure or failures and have made smaller, fewer ones. Prevision helps us prevent many failures. The more experienced in previsioning we are, the greater ability we have to provide, as we have more knowledge necessary to achieve previsions etc.. the more we can make accurate previsions, prevent many mistakes, failures, trouble, accidents, conflicts, arguments, unsuccessful actions, etc. In our personal and professional life, it is necessary to continuously develop and to have that personal goal to develop to a maximum capacity the prevision in private life, the ability to use previsions. We can continuously increase the capacity of our prevision very much, as we live if we have personal objectives, as we expand our ability to prevision and whether we act to continuously and effectively achieve this objective. Those who aimed at personal living as to develop the capacity of prevision continuously and concretely act with dedication to achieve their capacity to make a prevision which will help them achieve one or more very big successes, they will succeed to prevent many failures, troubles, etc., they will be able to achieve much in life, to have many happy, satisfying moments and so much happiness. The more we have a capacity of more than prevision, a more accurate, more efficient one, the more valuable we are for having this treasure. This treasure we can continuously increase greatly. The capacity of prevision generally contains more capacities of prevision in some actions, behaviors in the achievement of personal objectives, private, professional, specific ones, etc. It is necessary to develop those capabilities specific to prediction that we need. Knowledge, experience, qualifications, skills, etc., in a specific prevision capacity can be used to a greater or lesser degree in other capacities specific to prevision. The capacities of prevision are very necessary and very useful to us but unfortunately very few people have personal goals in life to continuously develop the specific performance of prevision. Due to the special importance of the capacity of prevision it is necessary and required to create and develop the science of the development of the capacity of prevision, because having this science we would have it by applying enormous positive effects on countless people that should develop and apply it indirectly on other people. The state would accelerate progress in many fields, would accelerate the reduction of illiteracy, poverty, illness, divorces out of arguments and conflict, accidents, what harms humans, animals, the environment, etc.. It would lead to solving many personal and state targets, it would create enormously many joys, much satisfaction and happiness. It would lead to the situation that most people no longer live at the whim of chance, with no personal, professional security, etc.. but on the contrary they would lead to more people having them as an objective and as they continue to live, they would develop the personal capacities necessary for their prevision and apply them every day, both in the establishment of private personal or professional life, it would be something concrete that will help them achieve more harmonious lives to achieve what they want and need for their families.

1020. There is the capacity of prevision in specific persons, specific societies, specific legal entities, nonprofit organizations, companies, banks, groups, collectivities, international and intergovernmental organizations. Both individuals and legal entities, must not live from hand to mouth, must act firmly, must study and evaluate the effects of positive and negative actions, decisions, etc. their objectives are also necessary to be: 1) to aim at continuing to develop their capacities of specific prediction that they need, 2) to apply, continuous use in any action, situation-specific prediction capabilities necessary and useful efforts, energy consumption and costs for the development and capacity of specific prevision that they need.

1021. Failures can happen in each of our actions or less often. Our failures can be created by factors and actions sometimes difficult to identify and prevent. However there are actions where we can know all the factors that can create failures. Knowing the factors that create failures in actions, we can take the necessary measures to prevent them by reaching in some cases to zero failures, as they have succeeded in situations in a long time, in many states, especially people in the most developed countries of the world. How to develop more this science with the more than we can know more of the factors that could cause failures in certain situations to certain actions. Scientific knowledge can contribute greatly to preventing many failures in many actions. At present people do not use scientific knowledge, the human experience gained in books, studies, on the Internet, although they have committed enormously many failures, mistakes, although they could prevent many huge mistakes, failures if they would use efficient, organized, timely human experience and knowledge from books, the Internet when they would need it. Countries should take immediate measures and be more interested in people and use them when they need knowledge and human experience that can reach and can be used. Human knowledge is growing and increases daily awfully much, and human experience which can create the situation so that we can prevent every day more even more mistakes and failures with positive effects on our high society, to accelerate progress in many areas.

1022. Where we have failures we should never discourage and lose our wits, our balance inside, our optimism, morale or to start to grieve. If we do this, it would solve absolutely no problem, but on the contrary, it would stress us illogically, abnormally without any positive effects. Those who have achieved many successes knew how to cope with failure, learning from failures, to reduce the negative effects of failures. Many failures rather than strengthening us, they weaken us, they should give us power instead of imobilizing us and mobilize us instead of making them harder to give motivation, instead of multiple negative effects they should have have multiple positive effects.

1023. However, I disagree and do not consider as logical, positive or constructive the popular saying: „Man learns from mistakes". Man, on the contrary should learn only from his successes and from those who have achieved successes and gained, by imitating those positive behaviors, which have effectively contributed to success. In addition man can learn enormously not to have failures, or make mistakes from the knowledge and positive experience of mankind stored in books, media, on the Internet and the experience of people who have huge experience and knowledge. The more we can prevent more failures, mistakes, the more we can prevent more and more different negative effects.

1024. It would be necessary and useful the development of a science to prevent human errors because it would prevent a large number of human errors and failures if people study and apply it as much and in as many actions as they can. This knowledge could and should be studied in colleges and universities and other educational forms. In every area of activity for each action type, it could identify factors that create human mistakes and failures and then it could identify solutions and measures to be taken to prevent mistakes and failures.

1025. Efforts and expenses that will be done by creating, developing, learning and applicating the science to prevent human errors will not be much lower than the positive effects of their prevention of a very large number of mistakes and failures and their multiple, diverse and very large negative effects. Financial investment, energy, time, etc.. in these activities related to the prevention of human errors and failures would be very effective and necessary and useful for both countries and for people in particular. Each of us in a greater or lesser way can participate in the creation, development and application of the science to prevent human errors.

1026. Member institutions, individuals, international organizations, nonprofit organizations, private firms, etc.. are necessary to carry out projects that lead to the positive use of knowledge of as many citizens of the world to achieve personal goals, whereas today it is basically used by very few people as compared to the world's population and very little knowledge of the existent one is used.

1027. The states of the world, the international organizations and institutes must identify the programs and projects of harmonious global co-development.

1028. The states of the world, the international organizations and institutes must create facilities to form efficient projects and programs of harmonious global co-development.

1029. Humanist economy would lead to preventing many international conflicts and wars.

Interracial

1030. Humanist economy will prevent many interracial tensions.

1031. Interracial tensions must be prevented in time.

Letting

1032. Persevering in not letting ourselves be stopped helps us achieve more pleasant surprises.

1033. The courage of not letting ourselves be stopped helps us achieve more successes.

1034. Persevering in not letting ourselves be stopped helps us achieve more efficient co operations.

1035. The ability of not letting ourselves be stopped helps us achieve more efficient co operations.

1036. Persevering in not letting ourselves be stopped helps us achieve more performances.

1037. Persevering in not letting ourselves be stopped helps us achieve much good luck.

1038. The ability of not letting ourselves be stopped helps us achieve more successes.

1039. The ability of not letting ourselves be stopped helps us achieve more favorable situations.

1040. The attitude of not letting ourselves be stopped helps us achieve more records.

1041. Persevering in not letting ourselves be stopped helps us achieve more personal goals.

1042. The courage of not letting ourselves be stopped helps us achieve more favorable situations.

1043. The attitude of not letting ourselves be stopped helps us achieve more successes.

1044. The courage of not letting ourselves be stopped helps us achieve much good luck.

1045. The courage of not letting ourselves be stopped helps us achieve more records.

1046. The courage of not letting ourselves be stopped helps us achieve more pleasant surprises.

1047. The attitude of not letting ourselves be stopped helps us achieve more performances.

1048. The courage of not letting ourselves be stopped helps us achieve more efficient co operations.

1049. The courage of not letting ourselves be stopped helps us achieve more performances.

1050. The attitude of not letting ourselves be stopped helps us achieve more favorable chances.

1051. The attitude of not letting ourselves be stopped helps us achieve more true friendships.

1052. Persevering in not letting ourselves be stopped helps us achieve more favorable situations.

1053. The ability of not letting ourselves be stopped helps us achieve more favorable chances.

1054. Persevering in not letting ourselves be stopped helps us achieve more records.

Lifestyle

1055. A great capacity of forming a positive own lifestyle must be developed.

1056. A great capacity of forming a positive own lifestyle helps us maintain our optimism.

1057. A great capacity of maintaining a positive efficient own lifestyle must be developed.

1058. A great capacity of forming a positive own lifestyle helps us achieve more favorable chances.

1059. A great capacity of forming a positive own lifestyle helps us become happy.

1060. A great capacity of forming a positive own lifestyle helps us become more optimistic.

1061. A great capacity of forming a positive own lifestyle helps us become productive.

1062. A great capacity of forming a positive own lifestyle helps us become practical.

1063. A great capacity of forming a positive own lifestyle helps us become optimistic.

1064. A great capacity of maintaining a positive efficient own lifestyle helps us become more loving.

1065. A great capacity of maintaining a positive efficient own lifestyle helps us become happier.

1066. A great capacity of maintaining a positive efficient own lifestyle helps us become productive.

1067. A great capacity of forming a positive own lifestyle helps us become more tolerant.

1068. A great capacity of maintaining a positive efficient own lifestyle must be maintained.

1069. A great capacity of maintaining a positive efficient own lifestyle helps us maintain our way of being understanding.

1070. A great capacity of forming a positive own lifestyle helps us become more cautious.

1071. A great capacity of forming a positive own lifestyle helps us become more loved.

1072. A great capacity of forming a positive own lifestyle helps us become wise.

1073. A great capacity of maintaining a positive efficient own lifestyle must be used.

Live

1074. Finding the meaning of our lives can be achieved also through the contribution of the formation, development, maintenance and usage of the humanist conception of life.

1075. Finding the meaning of our lives can be achieved also through the contribution of the formation, development, maintenance and usage of a legal conception of life.

1076. Finding the meaning of our lives can be achieved also through the contribution of the formation, development, maintenance and usage of an efficient conception of life.

1077. Finding the meaning of our lives can be achieved also through the contribution of the formation, development, maintenance and usage of a constructive life conception.

1078. A radical transformation of our lives for the better can be achieved also through the contribution of the formation, development, maintenance and usage of the ability to commit in everything we do.

1079. When you are in love and you are loved by the woman you love you feel truly alive.

1080. No one can describe the true happiness lived by that person who loves and who is loved by the person he loves.

1081. When you are in love and loved by the woman you love you live more intensely.

1082. No one can live the true happiness lived by that person who loves and who is loved by the person he loves.

1083. Nobody will ever have the ability to put on paper the happiness lived by that person who loves and who is loved by the person he loves.

1084. When you are in loved and loved by the woman you love you live more intensely.

1085. Those who have common sense deserve to live.

1086. True mature love lives on in time as long as the two lovers live.

1087. The one who truly loves and is loved by the very person whom he loves, feels really alive.

1088. When you are in love and loved by the woman you love, you feel the need to live forever.

1089. Those who live their life passionately and not at random have a greater ability to achieve their desired future.

1090. Those who live their life passionately and not at random have a greater capacity to succeed.

1091. Those who live their life passionately and not at random have the ability to achieve the social relations they desire.

1092. Those who live their life passionately and not at random have a greater ability to achieve a happy life.

1093. Our thinking can be made more efficient continuously for as long as we live.

1094. You are truly alive when you know how to live your life.

1095. Maintaining positive ambition must be a personal objective of ours for as long as we live.

1096. As long as we live we must develop our ability of changing our ideas from less efficient to more efficient.

1097. Who has hopes feels alive.

1098. Hopes have saved many lives.

1099. Hopes help us live more intensely.

1100. A man without hopes does not feel alive.

1101. The common values of friends increase the chances that their friendship last for as long as they live.

1102. Mutual love makes us feel alive.

1103. Only those who live a true mutual love know what that means.

1104. Women's hopes make them feel alive.

1105. A life in understanding makes us feel that we are truly alive.

1106. A life lived in a marriage makes us feel alive.

1107. Successes make us live life more intensely.

1108. True friendships make us feel truly alive.

1109. True friendships make our lives a lot more beautiful.

1110. Affectionate manifestations make the lives of lovers a lot more beautiful.

1111. Affectionate manifestations make the lives of spouses a lot more beautiful.

1112. Affectionate manifestations make the lives of lovers a lot more pleasant.

1113. Affectionate manifestations make the lives of spouses a lot more pleasant.

1114. Life is a lot more beautiful when you feel you truly live it.

1115. Life is a lot more pleasant when you feel you truly live it.

1116. Those who work with commitment feel truly alive.

1117. The common interests of spouses increase their chances to feel alive.

1118. AGC mediations help us change our lives for the better.

1119. Increasing the more useful usage of our time must be a personal goal of ours for as long as we live.

1120. Women must continuously develop, for as long as they live their inner beauty.

1121. Self-imposed discipline helps us become alive.

Majority

1122. Discrimination is one of the biggest causes of poverty for the majority of the people in the world.

1123. Schemers are rejected by the majority of people.

1124. Although the rules of success in life are very simple, they are not known, unfortunately, by many people. It is of course understood that those who do not know the vast majority of them will not have many successes.

1125. Even in 2007 in the majority of the states of the world so many incredible breaches of fundamental rights and freedoms of humans are made every day, unfortunately.

1126. Not even in 2007 the majority of states do not apply the most effective measures to prevent crime, unfortunately, but apply only primitive and inefficient methods of punishment through prison.

1127. The majority of employees who are well at work when they are offered another job they refuse.

1128. The majority of people with the sense of responsibility manage to achieve a beautiful life.

1129. Love for the vast majority of women is particularly important. Given this fact in having a relationship of true love, unfortunately, many facts are unacceptable.

1130. The majority of people want sincere friendship relations.

1131. It is necessary in the world's majority of states for the quality of lawyers to work up to the required level of reality, because there are possibilities to do so, but it is necessary to act in this regard.

1132. necessary in the world's majority of states for the quality of lawyers to work up to the required

1133. In 2007 the behaviors of the majority of people in the world are mostly selfish behaviors unfortunately. They are very harmful because these behaviors are particularly concerned with the interests of his own people, irrespective of the account that they damage other people and in some cases, exceptional people even die or huge damages are made.

1134. The majority of those with the sense of responsibility maintain mature love.

1135. The majority of those with the sense of responsibility achieve mature love.

1136. The majority of those who are very conscious most of the times self achieve themselves.

1137. The majority of those who are independent are hard workers.

1138. The majority of those who have the ability to consciously choose have a higher capacity to become more efficient.

1139. The majority of those who have the ability to consciously choose have a greater capacity to achieve outstanding performances.

1140. The majority of those who have the ability to react with understanding must be rewarded.

1141. The majority of those who have the ability to react with understanding have a greater capacity to participate in efficient global co operations.

1142. The majority of those who have the ability to react with understanding have more chances to achieve more and greater successes.

1143. The majority of those who have the capacity to react with understanding have more chances to achieve their personal goals.

1144. The majority of those who make true friends easily also have a good heart.

1145. The majority of those who easily make true friends also have more qualities among which human qualities can be found.

1146. The majority of those who easily make true friends also have a happy life.

1147. The majority of those who wonder without a purpose in life participate less to global humanization.

1148. The majority of those with the ability to react with understanding are appreciated.

Mentalities

1149. The negative mentalities of those who have them make it very difficult to achieve personal goals.

1150. The negative mentalities of those who have them make it very difficult to achieve efective co operations.

1151. If you unfortunately have some negative mentalities (which may be crimes) is good to stop their use.

1152. Negative mentalities make those who prevent them deserving to have some successes.

1153. Some behaviors, called mentalities, are not in fact mentalities, but crimes.

1154. If you unfortunately have some negative mentalities (which may be crimes) it is better to stop using them.

1155. Negative mentalities for those who do not prevent them keep them from having some successes that they could achieve.

1156. Negative mentalities make it very hard for us to achieve successes.

1157. Negative mentalities make it very hard to do effective actions.

1158. Those with negative mentalities do not achieve effective co-developments.

1159. Negative mentalities of those who have them greatly slow the achievement of personal goals.

1160. Negative mentalities of those who have them slow the achievement of effective co operations.

Misunderstandings

1161. Ignorance is a cause of many misunderstandings.

1162. Those with tact succeed in avoiding misunderstandings, conflicts, arguments, annoyances within the family.

1163. Each of the spouses need to always be calculated in family relations in order to prevent arguments, conflicts, misunderstandings etc..

1164. The tact of each spouse enormously helps them prevent many conflicts, arguments, misunderstandings, dispute and even divorce.

1165. Abstention is a quality, a behavior that is necessary for both spouses to have because abstention in situations that require the prevention of conflicts, they worsen the negative conflicts, quarrels, misunderstandings, disputes of marriage and sometimes even marriage itself.

1166. Through patience spouses manage to get to know each other better, accommodate with one another, to complement each other, to help each other to better understand themselves, to discover one another better, to overcome occasional misunderstandings between them, etc.

1167. Routine is very necessary and useful in behavior, etc. in actions for a certain period of time. After a certain period of time, at a certain time it is necessary to get rid of a certain routine, a certain behavior, a way of thinking, a certain kind of action, etc.. and replace it with another behavior more efficiently, more operational, more tactful, more thoughtful, etc.. in order to progress in achieving what we proposed, our personal objectives. When we need to get rid, to escape a certain routine it is necessary to get rid of it immediately, without doubts, delay, fears, etc. and to act in the new action, new behavior more effectively, without any delay. People who have the ability to leave a certain routine immediately when they need to, progress much faster in life, carry out much faster and more efficient personal goals, perform in live many more bigger or smaller successes than those who do not get rid of a particular or specific routine when necessary. Routine, when we get rid of it when necessary is a big negative factor of progress, it creates many failures, misfortunes, difficulties in achieving personal goals in life, it creates misunderstandings in families and may even lead to divorce, misunderstandings and even conflicts between large generations etc.. The routine of a normal fact, when we can not get rid of it, and it is necessary to get rid of it, it may actually become a very harmful fact for our new family, for the people around, for society, for younger generations and for the future, it may sometimes have many negative effects, very large and very diverse ones. For these reasons it is necessary to continuously develop our ability to get rid of routine when needed immediately.

1168. People who are also understanding manage to prevent many misunderstandings.

1169. Common values prevent many misunderstandings.

1170. We must never destroy a true friendship because of misunderstandings.

1171. Misunderstandings in true friendships must be resolved with tact in order that the friendship survives.

1172. Misunderstandings in true friendships must never lead to the destruction of that friendship.

1173. By preventing the formation of causes of misunderstandings we can prevent the apparition of misunderstandings.

1174. Misunderstandings can be avoided.

1175. Misunderstandings can be prevented.

1176. Misunderstandings must be prevented.

1177. A vigilant man has more chances to prevent many misunderstandings.

1178. The lost the behavior of a spouse with the other spouse can lead to more misunderstandings.

1179. By developing their inner beauty, women also develop their abilities that can help them prevent certain misunderstandings.

1180. Misunderstandings in marriages can be prevented.

1181. The art of solving misunderstandings helps us achieve more true friendships.

1182. Finding creative solutions that contribute to solving misunderstandings helps us achieve more favorable chances.

1183. The ability to solve misunderstandings helps us achieve more performances.

1184. The art of solving misunderstandings helps us achieve much good luck.

1185. The art of solving misunderstandings helps us achieve more records.

1186. Finding creative solutions that contribute to solving misunderstandings helps us achieve more efficient co operations.

1187. Finding creative solutions that contribute to solving misunderstandings helps us achieve much good luck.

1188. The art of solving misunderstandings helps us achieve more efficient co operations.

1189. Finding creative solutions that contribute to solving misunderstandings helps us achieve more records.

1190. The art of solving misunderstandings helps us achieve more pleasant surprises.

Necessity

1191. The gathering and storage of ideas in the bank of ideas is a vital necessity for the progress of mankind.

1192. Conflict prevention is a necessity for every one of us.

1193. Supporting positive action is a necessity.

1194. Popularization of positive actions is a necessity.

1195. Making peace is a necessity.

1196. Being healthy is a necessity.

1197. The spiritual development of each of us is a necessity.

1198. A necessity needs to be satisfied.

1199. Having a happy marriage is a necessity for both men and women and especially for children.

1200. Protecting people is a necessity and an obligation of society.

1201. Reading and studying books is a necessity and an obligation, we need to continuously achieve our objectives.

1202. Spiritual self-development is necessary, it is useful and it should become mandatory for each person as a personal goal due to the importance, necessity, utility, the requirement for spiritual development of each person of this planet, of countries and of all mankind. Spiritual self-development is a major highly efficient form of the development of our spiritual life.

1203. Involvement in positive activities is a necessity for all of us.

1204. Especially for the young true love is a particularly important necessity.

1205. The formation and development of the creative thinking of every person by the state is a necessity and an obligation of each state.

1206. Focusing on what we do is a necessity.

1207. The co-development of women and men is a necessity for society.

1208. Education for co-development is a necessity to society.

1209. Achieving a humanist society is a necessity for each country.

1210. Continuous self perfection is a necessity to succeed in life.

1211. Assuring personal freedom is also an individual necessity.

1212. The certainty of respecting human rights is a necessity for all states.

1213. Respecting human rights is a necessity for each individual.

1214. The state of certainty is a necessity.

1215. The certainty of respecting the human rights of nondiscrimination is a necessity for each state.

1216. Motivating people is a human necessity.

1217. The science of motivating people is a necessity.

1218. Humanist ideas are a necessity to people.

1219. Using our preventive thinking is a necessity.

1220. The sense of quality is a necessity.

1221. Constructive thinking is a necessity.

1222. Humanist ideas are a necessity for society.

Offenses

1223. Offenses may destroy many friendships.

1224. Sometimes, in a few cases from certain offenses, a family can reach a divorce.

1225. Some judges have done and made in their life, only through their participation in meetings of the court, more crimes than the total number of offenses prosecuted by them.

1226. Unfortunately, in many states there is still no justice, there is injustice, because the number of intolerable offenses, unlawful decisions pronounced which virtually surpass those just ones in some states.

1227. In anger many harmful offenses can be made.

1228. Repeated offenses between spouses can lead to divorce.

1229. Repeated offenses between friends can lead to the breaking apart of the friendship.

1230. Repeated offenses between lovers can lead to the destruction of love.

1231. Offenses can be prevented.

1232. Offenses between those who cooperate are very harmful to the cooperation.

1233. Offenses between those who cooperate can lead to the destruction of the cooperation.

Oneself

1234. Cherishing oneself helps us become active.

1235. A great capacity of being honest with oneself must be appreciated.

1236. A great capacity of being oneself helps us maintain our way of being loved.

1237. A great capacity of being oneself must be imitated.

1238. A great capacity of being oneself helps us achieve more pleasant surprises.

1239. A great capacity of being oneself helps us become more preventive.

1240. A great capacity of being honest with oneself helps us maintain our productivity.

1241. A great capacity of cherishing oneself helps us become productive.

1242. Cherishing oneself helps us become sturdy.

1243. A great capacity of being oneself helps us maintain our happiness.

1244. A great capacity of cherishing oneself helps us become more loved.

1245. A great capacity of being honest with oneself helps us maintain our way of being loved.

1246. A great capacity of being honest with oneself helps us become more humane.

1247. A great capacity of cherishing oneself helps us maintain our way of being liked.

1248. A great capacity of cherishing oneself helps us maintain our humanity.

1249. A great capacity of being oneself helps us become more enthusiastic.

1250. A great capacity of cherishing oneself helps us become more understanding.

1251. A great capacity of cherishing oneself helps us become more tolerant.

1252. A great capacity of cherishing oneself must be appreciated.

1253. A great capacity of being oneself helps us become efficient.

1254. A great capacity of being honest with oneself must be developed.

1255. A great capacity of cherishing oneself helps us achieve more performances.

1256. A great capacity of being honest with oneself helps us become happy.

1257. A great capacity of being oneself helps us become more productive.

1258. A great capacity of being honest with oneself helps us become more cautious.

Open-minded

1259. People who have had successes are mostly open-minded.

1260. Communicative people are more open-minded.

Opinions

1261. We are enormously wrong always when we hurry and give rash, hasty opinions in a dialogue.

1262. Spouses, even if they have different opinions, must understand each other.

1263. Lovers, even if they have different opinions, must understand each other.

1264. Friends, even if they have different opinions, must understand each other.

1265. Those who cooperate, even if they have different opinions, must understand each other.

1266. People, even if they have different opinions, must understand each other.

1267. A great capacity of having one's own principles and not letting one be influenced by the negative opinions of others helps us become more efficient .

1268. A great capacity of having one's own principles and not letting one be influenced by the negative opinions of others must be supported.

1269. A great capacity of having one's own principles and not letting one be influenced by the negative opinions of others must be formed.

1270. A great capacity of having one's own principles and not letting one be influenced by the negative opinions of others helps us become optimistic.

1271. A great capacity of having one's own principles and not letting one be influenced by the negative opinions of others helps us maintain our wisdom.

1272. A great capacity of having one's own principles and not letting one be influenced by the negative opinions of others helps us maintain our humanity.

1273. A great capacity of having one's own principles and not letting one be influenced by the negative opinions of others helps us become more preventive.

1274. A great capacity of having one's own principles and not letting one be influenced by the negative opinions of others helps us achieve more favorable chances.

1275. A great capacity of having one's own principles and not letting one be influenced by the negative opinions of others helps us become more understanding.

1276. A great capacity of having one's own principles and not letting one be influenced by the negative opinions of others helps us become cautious.

1277. A great capacity of having one's own principles and not letting one be influenced by the negative opinions of others helps us achieve more personal goals.

1278. A great capacity of having one's own principles and not letting one be influenced by the negative opinions of others must be maintained.

1279. A great capacity of having one's own principles and not letting one be influenced by the negative opinions of others helps us achieve more performances.

1280. A great capacity of having one's own principles and not letting one be influenced by the negative opinions of others helps us become happier.

Others

1281. I write to be useful and practical. He who writes every day to as many people as possible, helps them in one way or another, but as much as possible to help them achieve personal goals, brave performances, with strong will, with perseverance, to get as much satisfaction, joy and happiness as they can, to develop a harmonious personality, to be part of as much love for as long as they live, a happy family with happy children, to be hardworking, wise, to have harmony in the family, to have as many relations of friendship and cooperation as they can, to be what makes them better for their family, children and others.

1282. For those who have succeeded in life, who had one or more major successes, the effort they have made to pursue them without problems, to be consumed without having to make big efforts, they made such efforts on their own initiative, without them, someone would do them with great pleasure, without any stress, but it is considered that to succeed it is necessary to make those efforts, those actions. Although efforts, actions were very high, with huge consumption of mental and physical energy, more or less risks they felt of course, normal in order to achieve success, and what they proposed, and this is not to look at the facts not stressed, but on the contrary it has created a state of normality and even additional motivation and desire to do what they have proposed. These ones in contrast with others that the risky, unpredictable, great efforts chased, tried to solve, or attempted to carry out the enormous stress and had much inefficient behavior, but they always made them smarter, more effective, more operational, more powerful, more confident in their forces, in their success, in their future, etc

1283. We are very harmful in our struggle to become as rich as others. We need and must develop our positive parse, to fill the other etc. so that we can get much further than if we try to become another person.

1284. Pride departs the proud ones from others.

1285. It is necessary and required for states to take effective measures to prevent the formation, maintenance and development of all human vices, because they create enormously negative effects, both for those who have them, and for the others unfortunately.

1286. The cases of the bankruptcies of firms are innumerable, some of which may be known that the company will go bankrupt, others come from external factors that can not be controlled generated by us, such as bankruptcy has unexpectedly unite customers and no one can collect money from them any more.

1287. In life it is necessary and required to develop positive feelings just because they only do us and others good.

1288. Negative feelings harm both us and the others. Beware not to form, maintain and develop them.

1289. Each of us has the strength and will, if we want, to prevent the happiness, maintaining and development of negative feelings because they are extremely harmful to to us and others.

1290. Everyone is required to support the effects of their own mistakes and not try to do to bear others with them.

1291. It is illegal to try to make others responsible for your own failures.

1292. Some suicides are desperate acts arising from desperation, others are caused by some wrong ideas.

1293. In the world that exists on the Internet, in books, newspapers, media, databases and other information media there are enormously many positive ideas, helpful to people, to states but unfortunately many are not used by anyone, others are used by a tiny number of people as opposed to the number that could use and apply them.

1294. Egoaltruist behavior is a behavior that takes into account both the interests of the personal self, and those of others, acting to satisfy both, for a harmonious cohabitation for itself and for the other.

1295. My meditations push us, give us impulses to do only what is good for us, for others, and for society. Read, analyze them and apply those you accept. Good luck.

1296. The desire to obtain performance is necessary and must be positive for performance because it is good for some and unfortunately negative for others.

1297. Everything that does not harm others and is not prohibited by the law we can do it.

1298. To make others happy, it would be good that each of us gives a little happiness.

1299. It is necessary and we must never forget what tempts us harms us or others illegally.

1300. Those who have no sense alienate themselves from the others.

1301. You want to be respected, respect others.

1302. You want to be treated with common sense by others, and others treat you with common sense.

1303. Do not mock the others that you challenge them to mock you themselves.

1304. Leaders need to have a highly developed capacity and ability to understand others as well.

1305. A leader does not like to be a leader with great success only if it has qualities and abilities to understand others as well.

1306. He who has an emotional intelligence consists of: 1) the ability to understand others, 2) the ability to help others when needed, with ideas, solutions, and even financial and material ones, a service to resolve the problem, etc.. 3) the ability to see things from the viewpoint of others; 4) the quality and ability to solve problems through relationships that you establish with others; 5) qualities; 6) human qualities; 7) has a good control in any situation; 8) has the ability to easily interact with people; 9) has the capacity and capability to maintain human relationships; 10) has high qualities and abilities to motivate people to mobilize them to work; 11) has the capacity and capability to push people to achieve objectives; 12) has the capacity and capability to keep us optimistic continuously and in any event, and even in very difficult ones; 13) has the ability to never give up under any circumstances even if it appears to others without a way out 14) has high qualities and the ability to trust people; 15) has high qualities and abilities that people have confidence in him, in his qualities; 16) has high qualities and the ability for people to come to the opinion of a request in solving many problems; 17) has high qualities and the ability to gather people around him; 18) has high qualities and the ability to trust himself ; 19) has instinct; 20) is reliable.

1307. If you want to reach parliament, you'll definitely get in: 1) if you know how to solve efficiently and timely issues for people, 2) if you promise to solve the problems of the people, 3) if you understand people and their problems; 4) if you develop continuously and daily your capacity and ability to understand others and their problems; 5) if you have the quality and ability to see things from the viewpoint of others, people who want to vote for you and need you to solve problems; 6) if you have humane qualities; 7) if you have the quality and ability to interact easily with people; 8) if you have a high quality and ability to maintain human relations; 9) if you have a quality and ability to motivate and mobilize people to action; 10) if you have a high quality and ability to motivate people to achieve objectives; 11) if you have the quality and ability to be optimistic continuously and in any circumstances, even in they are very difficult; 12) if you have the quality and ability never to give up in any situation even if you have not succeeded very often in solving a problem; 13) if you have a high quality and ability that people have confidence; 14) if you have a high quality and the ability to trust people; 15) if you have a great quality and ability for people to come to you to ask your opinion in solving many problems, 16) if you have a great quality and ability to gather people around, 17) the great quality and ability to trust yourself; 18) if you have instinct; 19) if you are reliable, fair, honest, 20) if you have a great quality and ability to be optimistic in any situation , no matter how difficult it is, etc. If you do not have them it does not matter. It is learned through learning and continuous exercise. So if you want to be a parliamentarian, learn and practice those listed and you are surely to succeed. Good luck.

1308. The envy of the achievements of others is a very stupid thing.

1309. The envy of the achievements of others is a very large flaw, you should remove it as soon as possible because it harms us greatly.

1310. People with skills do not envy the achievements of others but appreciate them to just their value.

1311. Envy for the achievements of others destroys us on the inside like cancer harming us very much.

1312. People who are confident in others have faith in the global positive future.

1313. The man who is conscientious to positive influences achieves others in his life.

1314. Very giving people ready to interrupt their own road to help others have greater chances to achieve a more beautiful life.

1315. Very giving people ready to interrupt their own road to help others have the potential to become more efficient.

1316. My mediatations urge us to do what is right, what makes us, others and society better.

1317. Vanity removes those who are vane from the others.

1318. If we disturb others we will have many failures in life.

1319. Only activities as helping others take us towards achieving successes.

1320. Only activities as helping others take us towards achieving effective co operations.

1321. Negative actions always harm us and others more or less.

1322. Bad faith makes those who give evidence of bad faith be rejected by others.

1323. It is an absurdity. Those who are unfair towards others ask others to be fair with them.

1324. Hypocrisy alienates others from the hypocritical one.

1325. Rudeness removes us from the others.

1326. Revenge removes others from the vengeful one.

1327. Meanness causes others to depart from the mean one.

1328. Cruelty surely removes others from those who are cruel.

1329. Conceit removes others from the conceited one.

1330. Unscrupulousness removes the others from the unscrupulous one.

1331. Brutality removes us from others.

1332. Promptness in relations with others shows that we respect that person.

1333. Immorality makes the immoral ones be rejected by others.

1334. Every journalist has a great responsibility towards himself, towards others, towards society because of the possible impact of what he does, which may be a positive or negative case.

1335. It is unbelievable, but it is a reality. Some want to be respected but they do not respect the others.

1336. He who has no common sense has no respect for others.

1337. States have as a main objective, in addition to others, to ensure a quality of life appropriate for people.

1338. Unfairness removes the others from that who is unfair.

1339. Pettiness makes the petty one be rejected by others.

1340. Co-development helps to expand our capacity and power to better understand the others.

1341. The one who also has the qualities to motivate others to act with efficiency can produce more personal goals.

1342. Preventing premature actions helps us a lot more to prevent actions that adversely affect us and the others.

1343. Vanity pushes the others away from the vane one.

1344. By being patient with ourselves we will achieve efficient co operations with others.

1345. A man who is careless about himself and about others is dangerous.

1346. It is illegal to use others of our mistakes.

1347. Vanity removes the one who is vainglorious from the others.

Overcome

1348. Through a positive thinking we can overcome our desires.

1349. Flexibility in thinking and behaviors helps us surpass many hard to overcome obstacles.

1350. Through a positive thinking we can overcome envy.

1351. We can face and overcome difficulties much easier in life with the more we accumulate from books, the Internet; more useful and necessary knowledge for surpassing the troubles we face in life.

1352. Through patience spouses manage to get to know each other better, accommodate with one another, to complement each other, to help each other to better understand themselves, to discover one another better, to overcome occasional misunderstandings between them, etc.

1353. The more true the friends we have are, the more power we accumulate. This power helps us cope with the difficulties we have to overcome even the unfair hits we receive.

1354. If we are right, and have injustice in the law suits, it must give us greater powers to overcome injustice for us and to finally win justice.

1355. Adult love has the capacity and quality to face and overcome all obstacles and situations without exception of the two lives.

1356. Obstacles that stop us from achieving our personal goals can be overcome also through the contribution of the formation, development, maintenance and usage of the ability to be cooperative in activities.

1357. We can overcome the difficulties that we need to overcome also through the formation, development and maintenance of a positive enterprising spirit.

1358. We can overcome the difficulties that we need to overcome also through the formation, development and maintenance of quality in everything that we do.

1359. We can overcome the difficulties that we need to overcome also through the formation, development and maintenance of preventive thinking.

1360. We can overcome the difficulties that we need to overcome also through the formation, development and maintenance of the sense of fairness in everything we do.

1361. The limits of achievement imposed by ourselves in our heads at a certain moment can be overcome and eliminated also through the formation, development, maintenance and usage of the global thinking.

1362. The limits of achievement imposed by ourselves in our heads at a certain moment can be overcome and eliminated also through the formation, development, maintenance and usage of the sense of social justice.

1363. Those who have high objectives in life know how to overcome the dangers that come in life most of the times.

1364. People who have had successes have overcome the state of annoyance many times.

1365. People who have not succeeded in making a happy marriage must overcome the difficult moments.

1366. We can overcome difficulties that we must overcome also through the formation, and development and maintenance of efficient thinking.

1367. We can overcome difficulties that we must overcome also through the formation, and development and maintenance of the efficient co operations necessary in surpassing the difficulties that we are having.

1368. We can overcome difficulties that we must overcome also through the formation, development, maintenance and usage of the sense of self control.

1369. In order to change the desire of changing into reality it is necessary to form, develop, maintain and use the ability to know the difficulties that must be overcome.

1370. Our limits of achievement imposed by ourselves in our mind at a certain moment can be overcome, eliminated also through the formation, development, maintenance and usage of the ability to finalize ideas.

1371. Resistance to change for the better can be defeated and overcome also through the formation, development, maintenance and usage of the ability to be brave.

Participate

1372. People who take positive decisions can participate more rapidly in efficient global co operations.

1373. Some people with wrong ideas can not participate in global humanization because of some wrong ideas.

1374. The majority of those who wonder without a purpose in life do not participate in efficient co-developments.

1375. The majority of those who have the ability to react with understanding have a greater capacity to participate in achieving a positive global future.

1376. Those who control circumstances have greater capacities to participate in achieving the greater good.

1377. The sense of achieving quality in everything we do helps us participate more in global humanization.

1378. Calculated men participate in changing the world for the better.

1379. Persons who have no hopes, in order to create their hopes in the future, need to connect with people who participate in achieving efficient co-developments.

1380. Young man should participate all together in achieving the greater good.

1381. People with an innovating spirit have a great potential to participate in efficient global co operations.

1382. A man willing to try new ways is willing to participate in efficient global co operations.

1383. Those who know how to choose the road that suits them best have greater chances to participate in efficient global co operations.

1384. Those who have the sense of responsibility have a greater ability to participate in global humanization.

1385. Very sociable people are very willing to participate in achieving efficient global co operations.

1386. People with prejudices, because of some prejudices cannot participate in the way that they can to global humanization.

1387. People with wrong ideas because of some wrong ideas cannot participate in achieving the greater good.

1388. People with wrong ideas because of some wrong ideas than not participate in achieving the greater good.

1389. People who are confident in others have the chances to participate in efficient global co operations.

1390. There are a lot of skilled people who are unfortunately passive, do not participate in solving problems of the state.

1391. Those who have high objectives in life have great possibilities to participate in very efficient co operations.

1392. The uncertainty of incomes does not allow us to participate in some efficient global co operations.

1393. The capacity to form, develop and maintain only positive behaviors helps participate in achieving a positive global future.

1394. People who control their emotions have a greater ability to participate in achieving efficient global co operations.

1395. The uncertainty of incomes makes it hard to participate in some efficient co-developments.

1396. Most of those who wander without a purpose in life do not participate in efficient global co operations.

1397. The sense of achievement and quality in everything we do creates much more possibilities to participate in achieving efficient global co operations.

1398. Those who do not have hopes, in order to create hopes for the future need to connect with people who participate in achieving efficient global co operations.

1399. People who do not have hopes, in order to create hopes for the future, need to connect with people who have participated and who participate in global humanization.

1400. Those who control circumstances have a greater ability to participate in creating their future.

1401. People who have not succeeded in making a happy marriage must participate in global efficient co operations.

1402. Those who know how to take advantage of the opportunity of creation have more chances to participate in efficient global co operations.

1403. Those who know that discipline is one of the key of dreams participate more in global humanization.

Passivity

1404. Through passivity we can not progress.

1405. In life, through passivity and lack of activism we can not progress.

1406. Effective cooperation draws us out from the state of passivity and makes us more efficient.

1407. Effective co operations take us from the state of passivity and make us more efficient.

1408. AGC mediations help us get out of the state of passivity.

Peaceful

1409. Peaceful thinking prevents wars.

1410. Presently, mankind wastes its resources for negative activities such as: producing cigarettes, producing arms that exceed the necessary of solving problems in a peaceful way, maintaining overpopulated armies, maintaining repressive forces used exaggeratedly, etc.

1411. The judicial and criminal investigations must take place as peaceful as possible.

1412. A peaceful and reserved man has great chances to find his life partner.

1413. People who have success have peaceful relations with co-developers.

1414. It gives you great pleasure to be in the company of a peaceful man.

1415. Life is a lot more beautiful when it is surrounded by peaceful people.

1416. A peaceful man through his behavior contributes a lot to maintaining a happy marriage.

1417. In order to follow and transform our personal goals into reality, it is necessary to also form, develop, maintain and use our peaceful behavior.

1418. The radical transformation for the better of our life can be achieved also through the formation, development, maintenance and usage of peaceful behavior.

1419. Our happiness depends a lot also on the formation, development, maintenance and usage of peaceful behavior.

1420. Our own happiness can be achieved and maintained also through the contribution of the formation, development, maintenance and usage of peaceful behavior.

1421. Pessimism can be removed and replaced with optimism also through the contribution of the formation, development, maintenance and usage of peaceful behavior.

1422. Continuous self-control helps us become peaceful.

1423. Rather than lamenting that we do not have successes it is more useful to also form, develop, maintain and use peaceful behavior.

1424. We can overcome the difficulties that we must overcome also through the help of the formation, development, maintenance and usage of peaceful behavior.

1425. Continuously making ourselves efficient helps us become peaceful.

1426. Responsibility helps us become peaceful.

1427. Positive experience can be achieved also through the contribution of the formation, development, maintenance and usage of peaceful behavior.

1428. Hopes can be created also through the contribution of the formation, development, maintenance and usage of peaceful behavior.

1429. Wisdom helps us become peaceful.

1430. Self-imposed discipline helps us become peaceful.

1431. We can prevent the falling apart of a happy marriage also through the contribution of the formation, development, maintenance and usage of peaceful behavior.

1432. Confidence in ourselves helps us become peaceful.

1433. The force of our ideas can be augmented also through the contribution of the formation, development, maintenance and usage of peaceful behavior.

1434. We can form, develop and maintain the state of being ourselves also through the contribution of the formation, development, maintenance and usage of a peaceful behavior.

1435. We can become stronger and we can not allow ourselves to be influenced by the world also through the contribution of the formation, development, maintenance and usage of peaceful behavior.

1436. Creativity helps us become peaceful.

1437. Stress can be prevented also through the formation, development, maintenance and usage of peaceful behavior.

1438. Our resistance to changing for the better can be overcome also through the contribution of the formation, development, maintenance and usage of peaceful behavior.

1439. Hope helps us become peaceful.

1440. The limits of achievement imposed by ourselves in our mind at a given moment can be overcome or eliminated also through the contribution of the formation, development, maintenance and usage of peaceful behavior.

1441. In order to prevent not achieving our personal goals, it is necessary to also form, develop, maintain and use our peaceful behavior.

1442. Aspiring towards a more meaningful life can also be achieved through the formation, development, maintenance and usage of peaceful behavior.

1443. We can prevent some failures also through the contribution of the formation, development, maintenance and usage of peaceful behavior.

1444. Acting efficiently helps us become peaceful.

1445. Communication helps us become peaceful.

1446. In order to escape poverty it is necessary to also form, develop, maintain and use peaceful behavior.

1447. Cherishing oneself helps us become peaceful.

1448. Continuous self-motivation helps us become peaceful.

Peacemakers

1449. Wisdom helps us become peacemakers.

1450. Communication helps us become peacemakers.

1451. Acting efficiently helps us become peacemakers.

1452. Self-imposed discipline helps us become peacemakers.

1453. Continuous self perfection helps us become peacemakers.

1454. Continuous self-control helps us become peacemakers.

1455. The self efficient use of our time helps us become peacemakers.

1456. Creativity helps us become peacemakers.

1457. Cherishing oneself helps us become peacemakers.

1458. Will helps us become peacemakers.

1459. Confidence in ourselves helps us become peacemakers.

1460. Continuously making ourselves efficient helps us become peacemakers.

1461. Optimism helps us become peacemakers.

1462. Continuous self-motivation helps us become peacemakers.

1463. Responsibility helps us become peacemakers.

Persons

1464. Receptive persons achieve more easily their confidence.

1465. In order to achieve personal goals it is necessary to study how other persons have achieved the same personal goals.

1466. Each of us needs to prevent irresponsible behaviors as they are very harmful both to us and to other persons.

1467. Receptive persons have more chances to develop their trust in the future.

1468. Persons who are involved in projects have more chances to meet the right partner for life.

1469. People who are involved in projects have more opportunities to take more positive experiences from many persons.

1470. Some young people have a lot more experience, even if they are young, than many older persons.

1471. Luxury is very harmful for many persons.

1472. The need to succeed creates a more beautiful life for some persons.

1473. Persons who respect collaborators have more chances to achieve a mature love.

1474. Persons who take positive decisions have greater chances to achieve efficient co operations.

1475. Persons who take positive decisions use more information.

1476. Persons who take positive decisions contribute a lot in achieving a positive global future.

1477. Persons who take positive decisions have more chances to maintain a mature love.

1478. Skilled persons have a higher capacity to maintain true, mature love.

1479. The persons that take positive decisions must be promoted.

1480. People who have success are mostly not influenced by other persons.

1481. Persons with humane social behavior need to have a correct thinking.

1482. Happy marriages can be easily achieved because they only depend on two persons although the majority of people say that it is very hard.

1483. Humanist economy will continuously ensure workplaces and useful activities that are positive for all persons on the planet and it will eliminate and prevent unemployment.

1484. He who is very quiet hardly achieves relations with other persons.

1485. A quiet person gets into contact with other persons very difficultly.

1486. Very sociable and open persons have more chances of achieving efficient co-developments.

1487. Receptive persons have chances of becoming more performing.

1488. Very sociable and open persons have more chances of meeting favorable situations in life.

1489. Receptive persons have more chances to make more favorable situations.

1490. Persons with human social behaviors have a greater capacity to maintain a happy marriage.

1491. Persons who have no hopes, in order to create their hopes in the future, need to connect with people who participate in achieving efficient co-developments.

1492. Very sociable and open persons have much more chances of achieving mature love.

1493. Receptive persons have more chances to cooperate efficiently.

1494. Persons with human social behaviors must be appreciated.

1495. Persons who have no hopes, in order to create their hopes in the future need to connect with people who have the sense of commitment in everything they do.

1496. Persons who have not succeeded in building a happy marriage up to a certain date, in order to succeed they need to form and develop a correct thinking.

1497. Persons with human social behaviors must be rewarded.

1498. Persons who have no hopes, in order to create their hopes in the future need to connect with people who act efficiently to respect human rights.

1499. People who have not succeeded in creating a marriage up to a certain date need to come in contact with as many people of both sexes as they can who have succeeded in achieving happy marriages, in order to see and study how these persons have succeeded.

1500. Persons who have not succeeded in creating a happy marriage up to a certain date, in order to succeed they need to form and develop their affective soul's balance.

1501. Persons who have not succeeded in creating a happy marriage up to a certain date, in order to succeed they need to form and develop a greater ability to make positive changes in their personal life.

1502. Persons who have the ability to react with understanding also have the sense of fairness.

1503. The need to succeed sometimes creates, for some persons, great difficulties in achieving happy marriages.

1504. Persons with human social behaviors need to be also effective in positive actions.

1505. Persons with human social behaviors have a greater ability to achieve positive social relations.

1506. Persons with human social behaviors have more confidence in the future.

1507. Persons who have not succeeded in forming a happy marriage up to a certain date, in order to succeed they need to develop the ability of knowing how to motivate.

1508. Persons with human social behaviors must also have a positive thinking.

1509. Persons with human social behaviors have more qualities to achieve efficient global co operations.

1510. Persons with human social behaviors have more chances to find the right partner for life.

1511. True mature love makes some persons more optimistic.

1512. We must permanently be glad when we can help one or more persons.

1513. In some persons loneliness harms them a lot.

Potential

1514. Those who prefer unstoppable positive activism have a great potential to achieve themselves.

1515. Those who are emotionally balanced have a greater potential to achieve their future.

1516. Those who cherish their collaborators have a greater potential to achieve outstanding performances.

1517. Those who cherish their collaborators have a greater potential to achieve a happy marriage.

1518. Those who voluntarily assume certain risks only when they have an increased chance to reach their objective have a greater potential to achieve efficient human co-developments.

1519. Those who are enthusiastic have a greater potential to achieve a happier life.

1520. Our insufficient recognition is a potential factor of some failures.

1521. A man willing to try new ways has the chances and the great potential to achieve efficient co-developments.

1522. A man who approaches and is used to approach problems simultaneously from different points of view has the chances and a great potential to achieve a more beautiful life.

1523. A man open towards new ideas has much more chances and a greater potential to achieve a true mature love.

1524. A man who acts day by day, continuously to become even more efficient has much more and greater chances and a higher potential to meet even more favorable situations.

1525. A realistic man in interpersonal relations has much more and greater chances and a higher potential to achieve more true friendships.

1526. A man oriented towards the outside world has more and greater chances and a greater potential to develop efficiently.

1527. A man with imagination has a great potential to achieve efficient co-developments.

1528. A disciplined man has a great potential to increase his efficiency.

1529. People who are remarkably gifted have a much greater potential to prevent many mistakes.

1530. Those who are emotionally balanced have a greater potential to achieve efficient co operations.

1531. Those who build their life on rationally conscious bases have a greater potential to achieve personal goals.

1532. Those who have the sense of efficiency have a greater potential to achieve a more beautiful life.

1533. Those who possess the ability to dissociate emotions from their responsibilities have a greater potential to succeed in life.

1534. Those who possess the capacity to dissociate emotions from their responsibilities have a greater potential to contribute in achieving a positive global future.

1535. Those who cherish their collaborators have a greater potential to achieve more efficient co operations.

1536. Those who voluntarily assume certain risks only when they have an increased chance of reaching their objective have a great potential to achieve more efficient co operations.

1537. Ambitious men have a greater potential to achieve their personal goals.

1538. Ambitious people have a greater potential to become even more efficient.

1539. A man who approaches and is used to approach problems simultaneously from different points of view has great chances and a high potential to achieve his personal goals.

1540. A man satisfied with his own way of behaving socially has great chances and a high potential to achieve more and greater successes.

1541. A man open towards new ideas has more and greater chances and a higher potential to prevent many failures.

1542. A man who acts continuously, day by day, to be even more efficient has more and greater chances and a higher potential to achieve greater performances.

1543. A realistic man in interpersonal relations has much more chances and a greater potential to achieve a mature true love.

1544. Those who have had better social and economical conditions during their evolution have a greater potential to maintain their desired efficient co-developments.

1545. The need to succeed makes a man avoid much more potential mistakes.

1546. Those who discover unique ways to work efficiently for a better life have a greater potential to achieve outstanding performances.

1547. Those who control circumstances have a greater potential to achieve true friendships.

1548. Most of those involved in more projects have the potential to achieve efficient co-developments.

1549. Those who have had better social and economic all conditions during their evolution have a greater potential to maintain the desired true friendships.

1550. Spouses who value each other have a greater potential to have a happy family.

1551. A creative man has an even greater potential to become more efficient.

1552. Positive thinking helps us prevent many potential unpleasant surprises.

1553. Those who know that discipline is the key of dreams have the potential to achieve their own happiness.

1554. Positive ideas prevent many potential conflicts.

1555. Imagination can be developed with low psychical efforts but with potentially great effects.

Priorities

1556. Among the priorities of the world it is necessary to find the prevention and defeat of discrimination.

1557. Society, among its priorities should also have the following priorities:

1558. 1) To create the necessary institutions and to take the necessary measures to prevent with maximum effectiveness, efficiency and safety all the causes leading to the creation of situations where some people need human protection;

1559. 2) To create the institution: The Authority of Human Protection (1) to verify the state's institutions, individuals and private or illegal entities if they prevent the creation of the causes leading to some situations where people need human protection (2) and if they provide the human protection necessary for people who need this protection.

1560. We need to be permanently careful at how we order and reorder our priorities of personal goals.

Programs

1561. For our sake and that of others, of human society, it is necessary and required to appreciate, promote and apply positive programs and projects.

1562. Global humanist thinking will contribute greatly to the creation of very many global humanist programs and projects.

1563. States must unite and apply the harmonious global co-development thinking, must form programs and global projects of harmonious global co-development that are efficient and realistic.

1564. The states of the world, the international organizations and institutes must identify the programs and projects of harmonious global co-development.

1565. The states of the world, the international organizations and institutes must create facilities to form efficient projects and programs of harmonious global co-development.

1566. The level of situations and present technologies, the experience, the education, the resources of all kind allow and impose the development of harmonious global co-development thinking and the achieving of many global programs and projects.

1567. Harmonious global co-development thinking determines the participation in achieving many programs and projects.

1568. It is necessary to form and develop the science of continuous growth of the efficiency of using our resources at the global level, with the programs and projects of harmonious global co-development.

1569. Harmonious global co-development thinking, the projects and programs of harmonious co-development assure the development of personality.

1570. Humanist economy would develop many programs and global projects.

1571. Global positive human solidarity helps us a lot to achieve more humanist global programs and projects.

Progress

1572. The gathering and storage of ideas in the bank of ideas is a vital necessity for the progress of mankind.

1573. Idea banks are the most powerful engines of mankind's progress.

1574. Positive ideas are the engines of progress.

1575. Discrimination is very harmful to social progress, to all forms of progress.

1576. Peace was, is and it will be a factor of much progress.

1577. Perseverance is a factor of much progress.

1578. The irresponsibility of many people stopped in a lot of ways until now, progress in many areas.

1579. Young people from each state are required to become those powerful engines of progress, in general, and progress in every field including social, public administration, politics, as now they are not, unfortunately, in most of the world's states.

1580. The optimism of the young people is a very high energy of progress, but still insufficiently used.

1581. Considering a false value as a value is an enormous brake on the progress.

1582. Selfless deeds have contributed enormously to a lot of progress and outstanding achievements in all fields of activity.

1583. Scheming is destructive; it is a big brake on the progress in many areas.

1584. We can self-progress, continuously, day by day, if we set self-progress as a personal objective, for as long as we live.

1585. Day by day self-progress is necessary to become a personal objective, for as long as we live.

1586. Continuous, day by day, self-progress, helps us very much to achieve other personal goals.

1587. Spiritual self-development helps and contributes greatly to self-progress in other actions and activities.

1588. Moral limitation is a brake on the progress of the economy.

1589. The science of preventing human errors would accelerate progress in every field of activity.

1590. The spiritual continuous development of all people on the planet is one of the engines consisting of billions of engines that accelerate the progress of mankind.

1591. Prejudices hinder progress in many areas.

1592. Fear in a particular area of activity has hindered progress in that area.

1593. Optimism accelerates the progress of mankind.

1594. Due to enormous progress of human knowledge that is continuously growing daily, daily, the number of new opportunities to create a better quality of life is getting better.

1595. Futurology could help prevent the recurrence of many mistakes made so far and would achieve more progress in many areas much faster and could solve more problems more quickly.

1596. Women have made many outstanding deeds, have contributed enormously to progress in many fields, but from now on they will have a much greater contribution.

1597. Consensus is a factor of progress, success and performance.

1598. Through passivity we can not progress.

1599. Through solidarity we can achieve much more progresses.

1600. Seriousness is an earnest quality that helps us progress, keep our marriage, become happy, keep our friends and get more enjoyment and joys out of life.

1601. Every day we have the same 24 hours, but vary greatly according to the efficiency or inefficiency daily use of those 24 hours. Those who use it most effectively progress the most.

1602. Continuous self-learning helps us progress very much in life.

1603. In life, through passivity and lack of activism we can not progress.

1604. Creative thinking was, is and will be one of the main engines of progress in each area.

Public

1605. Young people from each state are required to become those powerful engines of progress, in general, and progress in every field including social, public administration, politics, as now they are not, unfortunately, in most of the world's states.

1606. Before publishing, those who write need to analyze the positive and negative effects of what they publicize.

1607. Each of us with the help of the qualities that we have with that of those that we can shape and develop, of the various resources around the world, of the human experience and knowledge acquired in books, on the Internet, in publications, etc. we can be optimistic in our future in achieving a happy future. It is necessary to mobilize the will, qualities given to us with all our being to achieve the personal goal of making a happier future for us. Good luck to all. The ideas exposed by me can help very much, use them.

1608. When we have a psychological fall, we become pessimistic at that time, etc.; in order to become as soon as possible more optimistic in problem solving, in the personal achievement of our objectives, it is necessary to talk to optimistic people on the

Internet or to read in books or on the Internet, in publications, optimistic ideas, ideas that can help us find solutions to resolve problems and achieve personal projects.

1609. To increase the number of people who will set as a personal goal the spiritual self-development and who will create greater opportunities for spiritual self-development to be done by as many people as possible who aimed for self-development as a personal goal, it is necessary to continuously create and develop the science of personal development which encompasses the spiritual and scientific personal self-development. Until we create and develop the science of spiritual development it is necessary to develop the science of spiritual self-development because so many people from many countries are more active and effective than the countries in which they live and thus they can be models for other people with positive models of personal self-development and so they can help them create and develop, achieve their personal objectives.

1610. Unfortunately, at present there is no science of spiritual development, no science of spiritual self-development, and there are not many people who have set the objective of personal spiritual self-development, although spiritual self-development is extremely necessary and very useful to each person and society as a whole. Because of these shortcomings and large utilities for its individual and society, it is very useful and very necessary that as many people as possible establish as a goal the personal self-development and have personal dedication to this goal for as long as they live to achieve themselves continuously and not wait until society or certain private or state institutions will create the science of spiritual development and the science of spiritual self-development.

1611. Spiritual self-development will help us greatly in spiritual development that can be accelerated if we continually study the issues that can help us grow spiritually, issues that we find stored in books, publications, television, on the Internet, in the life experience of people who have values and ethics and have achieved many and great successes thanks to the

237

development of their spirituality and ethic. The longer we self-develop spiritually the more opportunities we have to achieve more and greater successes that are made by spiritual self-development.

1612. The world's states have the obligation to regulate the registration on the Internet of court documents, of all acts of legal processes, files, everything that is public information, except for cases referred by law when the meetings are not public.

1613. Some forget that they must comply with laws even if holding public offices.

1614. The quality of justice would enormously increase if much more would regulate the court registration requirement and if all documents related to processes, files, everything would be public information, except for cases referred by law when the meetings are not public or on the Internet.

1615. The states' institutions need to manage the public money more carefully, more efficiently, more responsibility because now this leaves much to be desired.

1616. Consummer's Protection is required to extend its powers to check the activities of all state institutions that provide public services to citizens.

1617. Resolving problems between two people, of frictions between them through reproaches, in public, is not beneficial for any person.

1618. The quality of justice would grow enormously if states would legislate the obligation to record court sessions and all documents related to processes, files, everything that is public information except those situations expressly stipulated by the law when meetings are not published on the Internet.

1619. The world must legislate the obligation of putting recordings on the Internet of court sentences, of all documents related to the process, files, everything that is public information, except the circumstances stipulated by law when sentences are not public.

1620. People need and must act to sue all the elected and dignitaries, public clerks who do not respect their rights, who created damages.

1621. Corrupt politicians should resign by themselves from all public jobs.

1622. I feel a strong discontent when I see abnormality in public institutions' activities.

Reaching

1623. Each of us has had one or more bigger or smaller failures. It's good not to have any failures or as few failures as possible. Some or more failures could harm us very much. Those who were careful did not achieve failure or failures and have made smaller, fewer ones. Prevision helps us prevent many failures. The more experienced in previsioning we are, the greater ability we have to provide, as we have more knowledge necessary to achieve previsions etc.. the more we can make accurate previsions, prevent many mistakes, failures, trouble, accidents, conflicts, arguments, unsuccessful actions, etc. In our personal and professional life, it is necessary to continuously develop and to have that personal goal to develop to a maximum capacity the prevision in private life, the ability to use previsions. We can continuously increase the capacity of our prevision very much, as we live if we have personal objectives, as we expand our ability to prevision and whether we act to continuously and effectively achieve this objective. Those who aimed at personal living as to develop the capacity of prevision continuously and concretely act with dedication to achieve their capacity to make a prevision which will help them achieve one or more very big successes, they will succeed to prevent many failures, troubles, etc., they will be able to achieve much in life, to have many happy, satisfying moments and so much happiness. The more we have a capacity of more than prevision, a more accurate, more efficient one, the more valuable we are for having this treasure. This treasure we can continuously increase greatly. The capacity of prevision generally contains more capacities of prevision in some actions, behaviors in the achievement of personal objectives, private, professional, specific ones, etc. It is necessary to develop those capabilities specific to prediction that we need. Knowledge, experience, qualifications, skills, etc., in a specific prevision capacity can be used to a greater or lesser degree in other capacities specific

241

to prevision. The capacities of prevision are very necessary and very useful to us but unfortunately very few people have personal goals in life to continuously develop the specific performance of prevision. Due to the special importance of the capacity of prevision it is necessary and required to create and develop the science of the development of the capacity of prevision, because having this science we would have it by applying enormous positive effects on countless people that should develop and apply it indirectly on other people. The state would accelerate progress in many fields, would accelerate the reduction of illiteracy, poverty, illness, divorces out of arguments and conflict, accidents, what harms humans, animals, the environment, etc.. It would lead to solving many personal and state targets, it would create enormously many joys, much satisfaction and happiness. It would lead to the situation that most people no longer live at the whim of chance, with no personal, professional security, etc.. but on the contrary they would lead to more people having them as an objective and as they continue to live, they would develop the personal capacities necessary for their prevision and apply them every day, both in the establishment of private personal or professional life, it would be something concrete that will help them achieve more harmonious lives to achieve what they want and need for their families.

1624. There is the capacity of prevision in specific persons, specific societies, specific legal entities, nonprofit organizations, companies, banks, groups, collectivities, international and intergovernmental organizations. Both individuals and legal entities, must not live from hand to mouth, must act firmly, must study and evaluate the effects of positive and negative actions, decisions, etc. their objectives are also necessary to be: 1) to aim at continuing to develop their capacities of specific prediction that they need, 2) to apply, continuous use in any action, situation-specific prediction capabilities necessary and useful efforts, energy consumption and costs for the development and capacity of specific prevision that they need.

1625. Failures can happen in each of our actions or less often. Our failures can be created by factors and actions sometimes difficult to identify and prevent. However there are actions where we can know all the factors that can create failures. Knowing the factors that create failures in actions, we can take the necessary measures to prevent them by reaching in some cases to zero failures, as they have succeeded in situations in a long time, in many states, especially people in the most developed countries of the world. How to develop more this science with the more than we can know more of the factors that could cause failures in certain situations to certain actions. Scientific knowledge can contribute greatly to preventing many failures in many actions. At present people do not use scientific knowledge, the human experience gained in books, studies, on the Internet, although they have committed enormously many failures, mistakes, although they could prevent many huge mistakes, failures if they would use efficient, organized, timely human experience and knowledge from books, the Internet when they would need it. Countries should take immediate measures and be more interested in people and use them when they need knowledge and human experience that can reach and can be used.

Human knowledge is growing and increases daily awfully much, and human experience which can create the situation so that we can prevent every day more even more mistakes and failures with positive effects on our high society, to accelerate progress in many areas.

1626. Where we have failures we should never discourage and lose our wits, our balance inside, our optimism, morale or to start to grieve. If we do this, it would solve absolutely no problem, but on the contrary, it would stress us illogically, abnormally without any positive effects. Those who have achieved many successes knew how to cope with failure, learning from failures, to reduce the negative effects of failures. Many failures rather than strengthening us, they weaken us, they should give us power instead of imobilizing us and mobilize us instead of making them harder to give motivation, instead of multiple negative effects they should have have multiple positive effects.

1627. However, I disagree and do not consider as logical, positive or constructive the popular saying: „Man learns from mistakes". Man, on the contrary should learn only from his successes and from those who have achieved successes and gained, by imitating those positive behaviors, which have effectively contributed to success. In addition man can learn enormously not to have failures, or make mistakes from the knowledge and positive experience of mankind stored in books, media, on the Internet and the experience of people who have huge experience and knowledge. The more we can prevent more failures, mistakes, the more we can prevent more and more different negative effects.

1628. It would be necessary and useful the development of a science to prevent human errors because it would prevent a large number of human errors and failures if people study and apply it as much and in as many actions as they can. This knowledge could and should be studied in colleges and universities and other educational forms. In every area of activity for each action type, it could identify factors that create human mistakes and failures and then it could identify solutions and measures to be taken to prevent mistakes and failures.

1629. Efforts and expenses that will be done by creating, developing, learning and applicating the science to prevent human errors will not be much lower than the positive effects of their prevention of a very large number of mistakes and failures and their multiple, diverse and very large negative effects. Financial investment, energy, time, etc.. in these activities related to the prevention of human errors and failures would be very effective and necessary and useful for both countries and for people in particular. Each of us in a greater or lesser way can participate in the creation, development and application of the science to prevent human errors.

1630. Hopes prevent us from reaching the state of despair.

1631. The more effective actions we do are the more chances we have to prevent the situation from reaching despair.

1632. Good morale greatly increases our chances of not reaching the situation of despair.

1633. Effective co-development helps us a lot to prevent the situation of reaching despair

1634. Mature love helps us a lot to prevent the situation of reaching despair.

1635. Positive ideas help us a lot to prevent the situation of reaching despair.

1636. Forming, developing and using more and more qualities helps us prevent the situation of reaching despair.

1637. The more we have a proper education suited for our needs, the more chances we have of not reaching the situation of despair.

1638. The more we participate in effective co-developments the more chances we have of not reaching the situation of despair.

1639. An optimal morale increases our chances of not reaching the situations of despair.

1640. Optimism prevents us from reaching the state of despair.

1641. A happy marriage helps us prevent the situation of reaching despair.

1642. An optimal morale increases our chances of not reaching panic situations.

1643. Psychical balance increases our chances of not reaching situations of despair.

1644. Effective co operations help us very much to prevent reaching situations of despair.

1645. The more effective action we have, the more likely we are to prevent the situation from reaching despair.

1646. Those who have independence have more chances of reaching personal goals.

1647. Those who voluntarily assume certain risks only when they have a higher chance of reaching their goal have a greater potential to achieve a happy life.

1648. Those who voluntarily assume certain risks only when they have a higher chance of reaching their goal have more chances to meet more favorable situations.

1649. Today, we each have the happy chance of reaching world knowledge wherever we are on the globe.

React

1650. People who have the ability to react with understanding have more chances to achieve a happy life.

1651. People who have the ability to react with understanding are more humanist.

1652. Persons who have the ability to react with understanding also have the sense of fairness.

1653. People who have had successes have reacted with understanding.

1654. Most of those who have the ability to react with understanding solve problems through constructive methods.

1655. The majority of those who have the ability to react with understanding are humanist.

1656. People who know how to take quality decisions react with trust.

1657. Emancipation from self imposed restrictions can be made through the formation, development and maintenance of the ability to react with understanding.

1658. In order to pursue and transform our objectives into reality it is necessary to form, develop, maintain and use the ability to react with understanding.

1659. In order to take corrective decisions it is necessary to form, develop, maintain and use the ability to react with understanding.

1660. Abilities can be formed, developed, maintained and used through the contribution of the formation, development, maintenance and usage of the ability to react with understanding.

1661. Positive experience can be achieved also through the contribution of the formation, development, maintenance and usage of the ability to react with understanding.

1662. Rather than lamenting that we do not have successes it is better to form, develop and maintain the ability to react with understanding.

1663. Obtaining as many and great successes that we can can be achieved through the contribution of formation, development, maintenance and usage of a great ability to react with understanding.

1664. The state of psychical discomfort can be removed also through the formation, development and maintenance of the ability to react with understanding.

251

1665. We can overcome difficulties also through the formation, development and maintenance of the ability to react with understanding.

1666. In order to change our life it is necessary to form, develop, maintain and use the ability to react with understanding.

1667. The limits we have set can be overcome by the formation, development, maintenance and usage of the ability to react with understanding.

1668. Emancipation from restrictions can be made through the formation, development and maintenance of the ability to react with understanding.

1669. In order to pursue and transform positive objectives into reality it is necessary to form, develop, maintain and use the ability to react with understanding.

1670. The ability to react to understanding helps us achieve a happy marriage.

1671. The ability to react with understanding helps us become happy.

1672. The ability to react with understanding helps us achieve our personal goals.

1673. The ability to react with understanding helps us achieve effective co operations.

1674. The ability to react with understanding help us make more friends.

1675. We must know why we react like this.

Reasonable

1676. Reasonable men have more possibilities of maintaining a happy marriage.

1677. Acting efficiently helps us become reasonable.

1678. We can form, develop and maintain the state of being ourselves also through the contribution of the formation, development, maintenance and usage of a reasonable behavior.

1679. The necessary qualities in achieving personal goals can be formed, developed, maintained and used also through the contribution of the formation, development, maintenance and usage of reasonable behavior.

1680. In achieving our successes a contribution is also brought by the formation, development, maintenance and usage of reasonable behavior.

1681. Our resistance to changing for the better can be overcome also through the contribution of the formation, development, maintenance and usage of reasonable behavior.

1682. In order to prevent not achieving our personal goals, it is necessary to also form, develop, maintain and use our reasonable behavior.

1683. Self-imposed discipline helps us become reasonable.

1684. Stress can be prevented also through the formation, development, maintenance and usage of reasonable behavior.

1685. The obstacles that prevent us from achieving our personal goals can be surpassed also through the contribution of the formation, development, maintenance and usage of reasonable behavior.

1686. We can prevent some failures also through the contribution of the formation, development, maintenance and usage of reasonable behavior.

1687. The radical transformation for the better of our life can be achieved also through the formation, development, maintenance and usage of reasonable behavior.

1688. Problems cannot be solved by the ideas that created them but also through the contribution of the formation, development, maintenance and usage of reasonable behavior.

1689. The limits of achievement imposed by ourselves in our mind at a given moment can be overcome or eliminated also through the contribution of the formation, development, maintenance and usage of reasonable behavior.

1690. We can become stronger and we can not allow ourselves to be influenced by the world also through the contribution of the formation, development, maintenance and usage of reasonable behavior.

1691. Hopes can be created also through the contribution of the formation, development, maintenance and usage of reasonable behavior.

1692. We can prevent the falling apart of a happy marriage also through the contribution of the formation, development, maintenance and usage of reasonable behavior.

1693. Continuous self-motivation helps us become reasonable.

Rejected

1694. Schemers are rejected by the majority of people.

1695. A despicable man is rejected by people.

1696. The bastard man is rejected by the people.

1697. Luxury be rejected

1698. Lust is rejected by us all.

1699. Bad faith makes those who give evidence of bad faith be rejected by others.

1700. Those who are arrogant are rejected many times in many actions by those who are not arrogant.

1701. Immorality makes the immoral ones be rejected by others.

1702. Pettiness makes the petty one be rejected by others.

1703. Those who hate are rejected.

1704. Thanklessness makes those who are bastards be rejected by the others.

1705. Hypocrisy makes those who are hypocrites be rejected by others.

1706. People who are not careful with others are rejected.

1707. People who get annoyed often are rejected by people.

Relationship

1708. Spouses should not give up when dealing with troubles that appeared in the relationship between them especially because, many times, the solution is in front of them.

1709. Reproaches between spouses damage the relationship very much and does not resolve any problems but instead complicates matters.

1710. While entering into relationships with other people it is good to take from them as much positive experience and knowledge as we can because they help us achieve the happiness that we all want for ourselves.

1711. In life we can increase the chances of bigger or smaller successes through the implementation of effective relationships as many and as continuous as possible.

1712. The longer we are able to achieve more constructive human relationships, effective, harmonious ones, of mutual confidence, the more we will succeed more, the more certain we are to have a harmonious happy life, with more satisfactions, joy, successes and much happiness.

1713. The Internet is the ideal means to develop as many human relationships as possible.

1714. When we are depressed it does us good if we are in relationships with optimistic people.

1715. The depression of one of the spouses sometimes adversely affects family relationships.

1716. Good humor contributes in maintaining a relationship.

1717. Family violence of the husband against the wife made the relationship between spouses deteriorate very much.

1718. He who has an emotional intelligence consists of: 1) the ability to understand others, 2) the ability to help others when needed, with ideas, solutions, and even financial and material ones, a service to resolve the problem, etc.. 3) the ability to see things from the viewpoint of others; 4) the quality and ability to solve problems through relationships that you establish with others; 5) qualities; 6) human qualities; 7) has a good control in any situation; 8) has the ability to easily interact with people; 9) has the capacity and capability to maintain human relationships; 10) has high qualities and abilities to motivate people to mobilize them to work; 11) has the capacity and capability to push people to achieve objectives; 12) has the capacity and capability to keep us optimistic continuously and in any event, and even in very difficult ones; 13) has the ability to never give up under any circumstances even if it appears to others without a way out 14) has high qualities and the ability to trust people; 15) has high qualities and abilities that people have confidence in him, in his qualities; 16) has high qualities and the ability for people to come to the opinion of a request in solving many problems; 17) has high qualities and the ability to gather people around him; 18) has high qualities and the ability to trust himself ; 19) has instinct; 20) is reliable.

1719. A realistic man in interpersonal relationships should be valued, respected and rewarded.

1720. Love for the vast majority of women is particularly important. Given this fact in having a relationship of true love, unfortunately, many facts are unacceptable.

1721. It is much more pleasant to have sex with your partner than living in a temporary extra-conjugal relationship.

1722. Most of us do too little to maintain our health. This is a very big mistake which costs us many lives, reducing years of life, one or more diseases with more suffering, sometimes a happy marriage, good relationships with children, etc.. Attention to your health. Take sufficient care of your health. Good luck.

1723. Mature love exists due to the relationship between interpersonal love, mutual satisfaction of needs, objectives and personal expectations of the persons involved.

1724. Adult love is responsible, is based on logic, reason, mutual satisfaction of the need of love, lasting ties between the two lovers, confidence in one another, confidence in themselves, the success of their relationship and the achievment of personal goals, etc. .

1725. Love carries each of the parteners step by step through deepening mutual awareness, through the multitude of interrelations, through the needs to support the relationship in achieving personal goals, increasing confidence in one another, etc.

1726. The one who is testy destroys on its own many relationships of all kinds.

1727. For as long as we live we must seek to have relationships of friendship with special people, who have many successes, many qualities, many positive and effective

261

behaviors in order to learn from them as much as possible. This rule, this principle helps us achieve much easier and more personal goals.

1728. When you are depressed it does us good if we are in relationships with optimistic people.

1729. Senselessness in the relationship between spouses, if repeated, often leads to the destruction of the happy marriage.

1730. Mature love also contains relationships of mutual interdependence.

1731. The Internet helps us develop qualities of interrelationship. Use it. Good luck.

1732. The Internet helps us forge relationships of co-development with people at long distances.

1733. Mental discomfort present to those who cooperate, created by the relationships between those who cooperate greatly reduces the effectiveness of the cooperation.

1734. Unfortunately, a number of lawyers should be behind bars because of the many crimes they have done, because of the misfortunes and damage they have done, because of illegal behaviors in their relationship with their clients.

1735. Spouses need to agree in what there will be in their relationships with children, to have an equal behavior in order not to damage any children or relations between them.

1736. Hatred makes relationships between people worse.

1737. Good mood can be achieved if the person concerned has adequate nourishment, it can be achieved through education, intellectual work, perseverance, willpower, exercise, a value system that we believe in and that we respect, business dynamism, social relationships, friends, mature love and a happy marriage.

1738. Men who have relationships with women with higher incomes than them must not feel like that is a complex.

1739. He who barely maintains a relationship makes true friends very hard.

1740. A realistic man in personal relationships has more chances and a greater potential to achieve a happy life.

1741. Ignoring the truth contributes a lot to breaking many relationships.

1742. People who have not succeeded in achieving a happy marriage up to a certain date, in order to succeed they need to form and develop the necessary qualities to achieve and maintain a balanced love relationship.

1743. The game of seduction helps us achieve love relationships.

1744. The realistic man in interpersonal relationships is more likely to achieve his personal goals.

1745. Successful relationships can be achieved step by step and with perseverance.

1746. The more inter human effective relationships we have the more chances we have to progress in life a lot faster.

1747. Inter human effective relationships can be formed, they are not just given.

1748. Arrogance is very harmful to inter-human relationships.

Respecting

1749. By acting, respecting the rules to becoming happy, we become happy

1750. We can make life happier by respecting the rules that make our life happier.

1751. We can build our happiness by respecting those principles that lead us to happiness.

1752. We can only build happiness by respecting those principles that lead us to happiness.

1753. Respecting people gives us increased credibility.

1754. Respecting principles helps us achieve efficient co-developments.

1755. Respecting principles helps us maintain a happy marriage.

1756. Respecting principles helps us become more efficient.

1757. Respecting principles helps us maintain true friendships.

1758. Respecting principles helps us maintain efficient co operations.

1759. The certainty of respecting human rights is a necessity for all states.

1760. The certainty of respecting human rights is an obligation for all states.

1761. Respecting human rights is a necessity for each individual.

1762. Respecting human rights is an obligation for each person.

1763. Not respecting human rights is a serious abuse done by states.

1764. The certainty of respecting the human rights of nondiscrimination is a necessity for each state.

1765. The certainty of respecting the rights to non discrimination of people is an obligation for each state.

1766. Not respecting the right to nondiscrimination of people by the state is a great abuse.

1767. Respecting the right to nondiscrimination of people is mandatory for each person of the planet.

1768. Respecting the right to nondiscrimination of people contributes a lot to preventing many conflicts.

1769. Respecting promises makes us more credible.

1770. Respecting promises helps us achieve more and greater successes.

1771. Respecting collaborators is a mutual obligation of the associates.

1772. Respecting each person's collaborator is a principle of collaboration.

1773. Respecting one's collaborator is an obligation.

1774. Respecting one's collaborator is a necessity.

1775. The safety of respecting human rights is a necessity for each state.

1776. Respecting your collaborators is a necessity.

1777. Those who do not have hopes, in order to create hopes for the future need to connect with people who act efficiently and not out of respecting the rights.

1778. Respecting your collaborator is his right.

Rights

1779. An official who does not respect human rights should be dismissed immediately.

1780. Judges which during their professional activity have committed breaches of human rights must necessarily give their resignation themselves.

1781. Young people from all states in the world who are marginalized, not taken into account, it is necessary to act, to be organized in NGOs, trade unions, political parties and other institutions, to act with efficiency and effectively to promote and support the rights and interests that their leadership is found in administration councils, local and central state, parliaments, local governments, etc..

1782. Most world members do very little and ineffective things to prevent the disregard of rights and fundamental freedoms.

1783. Even in 2007 in the majority of the states of the world so many incredible breaches of fundamental rights and freedoms of humans are made every day, unfortunately.

1784. All world members need to take all necessary and effective measures to stop immediately and effectively all disregards of rights and fundamental freedoms.

1785. For all young people it is necessary and required to work continuously to defend their rights until they are complied with all the rights.

1786. Young people should be more united in the action to defend their rights.

1787. Young people must not remain passive in the face of the disrespect of their rights.

1788. Young people who are careless when their rights are unobserved make very big mistakes.

1789. Life for many people had been and would be more beautiful if they did not receive the violation of human rights by the court.

1790. All young people need and must learn to defend their rights.

1791. The young, when they have unobserved rights, must unite and act for their rights to be respected.

1792. Respect for human rights must be one of the objectives of each state.

1793. Each of us is required to have as a personal goal the respect of human rights of the other, continuously, day by day, for as long as we live.

1794. Co-development thinking is more effective because it implies two or more persons, also regarding the rights and needs of everyone.

1795. The world's states have sufficient resources to stop felonies and end the noncompliance with the fundamental rights and freedoms of man, but unfortunately they do not take any measures in this purpose.

1796. Unfortunately in most of the world states there are still illegal court orders that do not respect human rights.

1797. Most world states work very little and ineffectively to prevent the disregard for human rights and fundamental freedoms.

1798. Unfortunately in 2007 in most states of the world there are still every day so many incredible violations of the human rights and fundamental freedoms.

1799. All the states in the world need to take all necessary and effective measures to immediately and effectively stop any violation of human rights and fundamental freedoms.

1800. People need and must act to sue all the elected and dignitaries, public clerks who do not respect their rights, who created damages.

1801. The certainty of respecting human rights is a necessity for all states.

1802. The certainty of respecting human rights is an obligation for all states.

1803. Respecting human rights is a necessity for each individual.

1804. Respecting human rights is an obligation for each person.

1805. Not respecting human rights is a serious abuse done by states.

1806. Each state is obligated to take the necessary measures to prevent all forms of non compliance with human rights.

1807. The certainty of respecting the human rights of nondiscrimination is a necessity for each state.

1808. The certainty of respecting the rights to non discrimination of people is an obligation for each state.

1809. The freedom of speech must respect human rights.

1810. The safety of respecting human rights is a necessity for each state.

1811. People with human social behaviors need to act in order to respect human rights.

1812. Persons who have no hopes, in order to create their hopes in the future need to connect with people who act efficiently to respect human rights.

1813. Those who do not have hopes, in order to create hopes for the future need to act to respect human rights.

1814. Those who do not have hopes, in order to create hopes for the future need to connect with people who act efficiently and not out of respecting the rights.

1815. Those who do not have hopes, in order to create hopes for the future they need to act to respect rights.

1816. Constructive thinking does not accept the non-abiding of human rights.

1817. People with human social behaviors need to act in order to respect the rights for nondiscrimination.

United Nations Organization Universal Declaration of Human Rights.

Article 1.

- All human beings are born free and equal in dignity and rights.They are endowed with reason and conscience and should act towards one another in a spirit of brotherhood.

Article 2.

- Everyone is entitled to all the rights and freedoms set forth in this Declaration, without distinction of any kind, such as race, colour, sex, language, religion, political or other opinion, national or social origin, property, birth or other status. Furthermore, no distinction shall be made on the basis of the political, jurisdictional or international status of the country or territory to which a person belongs, whether it be independent, trust, non-self-governing or under any other limitation of sovereignty.

Article 3.

- Everyone has the right to life, liberty and security of person.

Article 4.

- No one shall be held in slavery or servitude; slavery and the slave trade shall be prohibited in all their forms.

Article 5.

- No one shall be subjected to torture or to cruel, inhuman or degrading treatment or punishment.

Article 6.

- Everyone has the right to recognition everywhere as a person before the law.

Article 7.

- All are equal before the law and are entitled without any discrimination to equal protection of the law. All are entitled to equal protection against any discrimination in violation of this Declaration and against any incitement to such discrimination.

Article 8.

- Everyone has the right to an effective remedy by the competent national tribunals for acts violating the fundamental rights granted him by the constitution or by law.

Article 9.

- No one shall be subjected to arbitrary arrest, detention or exile.

Article 10.

- Everyone is entitled in full equality to a fair and public hearing by an independent and impartial tribunal, in the determination of his rights and obligations and of any criminal charge against him.

Article 11.

- (1) Everyone charged with a penal offence has the right to be presumed innocent until proved guilty according to law in a public trial at which he has had all the guarantees necessary for his defence.
- (2) No one shall be held guilty of any penal offence on account of any act or omission

which did not constitute a penal offence, under national or international law, at the time when it was committed. Nor shall a heavier penalty be imposed than the one that was applicable at the time the penal offence was committed.

Article 12.

- No one shall be subjected to arbitrary interference with his privacy, family, home or correspondence, nor to attacks upon his honour and reputation. Everyone has the right to the protection of the law against such interference or attacks.

Article 13.

- (1) Everyone has the right to freedom of movement and residence within the borders of each state.
- (2) Everyone has the right to leave any country, including his own, and to return to his country.

Article 14.

- (1) Everyone has the right to seek and to enjoy in other countries asylum from persecution.
- (2) This right may not be invoked in the case of prosecutions genuinely arising from non-political crimes or from acts contrary to the purposes and principles of the United Nations.

Article 15.

- (1) Everyone has the right to a nationality.
- (2) No one shall be arbitrarily deprived of his nationality nor denied the right to change his nationality.

Article 16.

- (1) Men and women of full age, without any limitation due to race, nationality or religion, have the right to marry and to found a family. They are entitled to equal rights as to marriage, during marriage and at its dissolution.
- (2) Marriage shall be entered into only with the free and full consent of the intending spouses.
- (3) The family is the natural and fundamental group unit of society and is

entitled to protection by society and the State.

Article 17.

- (1) Everyone has the right to own property alone as well as in association with others.
- (2) No one shall be arbitrarily deprived of his property.

Article 18.

- Everyone has the right to freedom of thought, conscience and religion; this right includes freedom to change his religion or belief, and freedom, either alone or in community with others and in public or private, to manifest his religion or belief in teaching, practice, worship and observance.

Article 19.

- Everyone has the right to freedom of opinion and expression; this right includes freedom to hold opinions without interference and to seek, receive and impart information and ideas through any media and regardless of frontiers.

Article 20.

- (1) Everyone has the right to freedom of peaceful assembly and association.
- (2) No one may be compelled to belong to an association.

Article 21.

- (1) Everyone has the right to take part in the government of his country, directly or through freely chosen representatives.
- (2) Everyone has the right of equal access to public service in his country.
- (3) The will of the people shall be the basis of the authority of government; this will shall be expressed in periodic and genuine elections which shall be by universal and equal suffrage and shall be held by secret vote or by equivalent free voting procedures.

Article 22.

- Everyone, as a member of society, has the right to social security and is entitled to realization, through national effort and international co-operation and in accordance with the organization and resources of each State, of the economic, social and cultural rights indispensable for his dignity and the free development of his personality.

Article 23.

- (1) Everyone has the right to work, to free choice of employment, to just and favourable conditions of work and to protection against unemployment.
- (2) Everyone, without any discrimination, has the right to equal pay for equal work.
- (3) Everyone who works has the right to just and favourable remuneration ensuring for himself and his family an existence worthy of human dignity, and supplemented, if necessary, by other means of social protection.
- (4) Everyone has the right to form and to join trade unions for the protection of his interests.

Article 24.

- Everyone has the right to rest and leisure, including reasonable limitation of working hours and periodic holidays with pay.

Article 25.

- (1) Everyone has the right to a standard of living adequate for the health and well-being of himself and of his family, including food, clothing, housing and medical care and necessary social services, and the right to security in the event of unemployment, sickness, disability, widowhood, old age or other lack of livelihood in circumstances beyond his control.
- (2) Motherhood and childhood are entitled to special care and assistance. All children, whether born in or out of wedlock, shall enjoy the same social protection.

Article 26.

- (1) Everyone has the right to education. Education shall be free, at least in the elementary and fundamental stages. Elementary education shall be compulsory. Technical and professional education shall be made generally available and higher education shall be equally accessible to all on the basis of merit.
- (2) Education shall be directed to the full development of the human personality and to the strengthening of respect for human rights and fundamental freedoms. It shall

promote understanding, tolerance and friendship among all nations, racial or religious groups, and shall further the activities of the United Nations for the maintenance of peace.

- (3) Parents have a prior right to choose the kind of education that shall be given to their children.

Article 27.

- (1) Everyone has the right freely to participate in the cultural life of the community, to enjoy the arts and to share in scientific advancement and its benefits.
- (2) Everyone has the right to the protection of the moral and material interests resulting from any scientific, literary or artistic production of which he is the author.

Article 28.

- Everyone is entitled to a social and international order in which the rights and freedoms set forth in this Declaration can be fully realized.

Article 29.

- (1) Everyone has duties to the community in which alone the free and full development of his personality is possible.
- (2) In the exercise of his rights and freedoms, everyone shall be subject only to such limitations as are determined by law solely for the purpose of securing due recognition and respect for the rights and freedoms of others and of meeting the just requirements of morality, public order and the general welfare in a democratic society.
- (3) These rights and freedoms may in no case be exercised contrary to the purposes and principles of the United Nations.

Article 30.

- Nothing in this Declaration may be interpreted as implying for any State, group or person any right to engage in any activity or to perform any act aimed at the destruction of any of the rights and freedoms set forth herein.

Member states of the United Nations Organization.

- A

- •
- Afghanistan
- 19-11-1946

- •
- Albania
- 14-12-1955

- •
- Algeria
- 08-10-1962

- •
- Andorra
- 28-07-1993

- •
- Angola
- 01-12-1976

- •
- Antigua and Barbuda
- 11-11-1981

- •
- Argentina

- • 24-10-1945

- •
- Armenia
- 02-03-1992

- •
- Australia
- 01-11-1945

- •
- Austria
- 14-12-1955

- •
- Azerbaijan
- 02-03-1992

- •

- B

-

- •
- Bahamas
- 18-09-1973

285

- •
- Bahrain
- 21-09-1971

- •
- Bangladesh
- 17-09-1974

- •
- Barbados
- 09-12-1966

- •
- Belarus*
- 24-10-1945

- •
- Belgium
- 27-12-1945

- •
- Belize
- 25-09-1981

- •
- Benin
- 20-09-1960

- •
- Bhutan
- 21-09-1971

- •

- • Bolivia (Plurinational State of)
- 14-11-1945

- •
- Bosnia and Herzegovina*
- 22-05-1992

- •
- Botswana
- 17-10-1966

- •
- Brazil
- 24-10-1945

- •
- Brunei Darussalam
- 21-09-1984

- •
- Bulgaria
- 14-12-1955

- •
- Burkina Faso
- 20-09-1960

- •
- Burundi
- 18-09-1962

- •

C

- ▲

- •
- Cambodia
- 14-12-1955

- •
- Cameroon
- 20-09-1960

- •
- Canada
- 09-11-1945

- •
- Cape Verde
- 16-09-1975

- •
- Central African Republic
- 20-09-1960

- •
- Chad
- 20-09-1960

- •
- Chile

- • 24-10-1945

- •
- China
- 24-10-1945

- •
- Colombia
- 05-11-1945

- •
- Comoros
- 12-11-1975

- •
- Congo
- 20-09-1960

- •
- Costa Rica
- 02-11-1945

- •
- Côte D'Ivoire
- 20-09-1960

- •
- Croatia*
- 22-05-1992

- •
- Cuba
- 24-10-1945

287

- •
- Cyprus
- 20-09-1960

- •
- Czech Republic[*]
- 19-01-1993

- •

D

- ▲

- •
- Democratic People's Republic of Korea
- 17-09-1991

- •
- Democratic Republic of the Congo[*]
- 20-09-1960

- •
- Denmark
- 24-10-1945

- •
- Djibouti
- 20-09-1977

- •

- Dominica
- 18-12-1978

- •
- Dominican Republic
- 24-10-1945

- •

E

- ▲

- •
- Ecuador
- 21-12-1945

- •
- Egypt[*]
- 24-10-1945

- •
- El Salvador
- 24-10-1945

- •
- Equatoral Guinea
- 12-11-1968

- •
- Eritrea
- 28-05-1993

288

- •
- Estonia
- 17-09-1991

- •
- Ethiopia
- 13-11-1945

- •

F

-

- •
- Fiji
- 13-10-1970

- •
- Finland
- 14-12-1955

- •
- France
- 24-10-1945

- •

G

-

- •

- Gabon
- 20-09-1960

- •
- Gambia
- 21-09-1965

- •
- Georgia
- 31-07-1992

- •
- Germany[*]
- 18-09-1973

- •
- Ghana
- 08-03-1957

- •
- Greece
- 25-10-1945

- •
- Grenada
- 17-09-1974

- •
- Guatemala
- 21-11-1945

- •
- Guinea

289

- 12-12-1958

- •
- Guinea Bissau
- 17-09-1974

- •
- Guyana
- 20-09-1966

- •

H

- •

- •
- Haiti
- 24-10-1945

- •
- Honduras
- 17-12-1945

- •
- Hungary
- 14-12-1955

- •

I

- •

- •
- Iceland
- 19-11-1946

- •
- India
- 30-10-1945

- •
- Indonesia[*]
- 28-09-1950

- •
- Iran (Islamic Republic of)
- 24-10-1945

- •
- Iraq
- 21-12-1945

- •
- Ireland
- 14-12-1955

- •
- Israel
- 11-05-1949

- •
- Italy
- 14-12-1955

J

Jamaica
18-09-1962

Japan
18-12-1956

Jordan
14-12-1955

K

Kazakhstan
02-03-1992

Kenya
16-12-1963

Kiribati
14-09-1999

Kuwait
14-05-1963

Kyrgyzstan
02-03-1992

L

Lao People's
Democratic Republic
14-12-1955

Latvia
17-09-1991

Lebanon
24-10-1945

Lesotho
17-10-1966

- Liberia
- 02-11-1945

- Libyan Arab Jamahiriya
- 14-12-1955

- Liechtenstein
- 18-09-1990

- Lithuania
- 17-09-1991

- Luxembourg
- 24-10-1945

-

M

-

- Madagascar
- 20-09-1960

- Malawi

- 01-12-1964

- Malaysia[*]
- 17-09-1957

- Maldives
- 21-09-1965

- Mali
- 28-09-1960

- Malta
- 01-12-1964

- Marshall Islands
- 17-09-1991

- Mauritania
- 27-10-1961

- Mauritius
- 24-04-1968

- Mexico
- 07-11-1945

- -
- Micronesia, Federated States of
- 17-09-1991

- -
- Monaco
- 28-05-1993

- -
- Mongolia
- 27-10-1961

- -
- Montenegro[*]
- 28-06-2006

- -
- Morocco
- 12-11-1956

- -
- Mozambique
- 16-09-1975

- -
- Myanmar
- 19-04-1948

- -

N

- -

- -
- Namibia
- 23-04-1990

- -
- Nauru
- 14-09-1999

- -
- Nepal
- 14-12-1955

- -
- Netherlands
- 10-12-1945

- -
- New Zealand
- 24-10-1945

- -
- Nicaragua
- 24-10-1945

- -
- Niger
- 20-09-1960

- -
- Nigeria
- 07-10-1960

293

- •
- Norway
- 27-11-1945

- •

O

- •

- •
- Oman
- 07-10-1971

- •

P

- •

- •
- Pakistan
- 30-09-1947

- •
- Palau
- 15-12-1994

- •
- Panama
- 13-11-1945

- •

- Papua New Guinea
- 10-10-1975

- •
- Paraguay
- 24-10-1945

- •
- Peru
- 31-10-1945

- •
- Philippines
- 24-10-1945

- •
- Poland
- 24-10-1945

- •
- Portugal
- 14-12-1955

- •

Q

- •

- •
- Qatar
- 21-09-1971

- •

R

-

- •
- Republic of Korea
- 17-09-1991

- •
- Republic of Moldova
- 02-03-1992

- •
- Romania
- 14-12-1955

- •
- Russian Federation*
- 24-10-1945

- •
- Rwanda
- 18-09-1962

- •

S

-

- •

- Saint Kitts and Nevis
- 23-09-1983

- •
- Saint Lucia
- 18-09-1979

- •
- Saint Vincent and the Grenadines
- 16-09-1980

- •
- Samoa
- 15-12-1976

- •
- San Marino
- 02-03-1992

- •
- Sao Tome and Principe
- 16-09-1975

- •
- Saudi Arabia
- 24-10-1945

- •
- Senegal
- 28-09-1960

- •

- Serbia[*]
- 01-11-2000

- •
- Seychelles
- 21-09-1976

- •
- Sierra Leone
- 27-09-1961

- •
- Singapore[*]
- 21-09-1965

- •
- Slovakia[*]
- 19-01-1993

- •
- Slovenia[*]
- 22-05-1992

- •
- Solomon Islands
- 19-09-1978

- •
- Somalia
- 20-09-1960

- •
- South Africa

- 07-11-1945

- •
- Spain
- 14-12-1955

- •
- Sri Lanka
- 14-12-1955

- •
- Sudan
- 12-11-1956

- •
- Suriname
- 04-12-1975

- •
- Swaziland
- 24-09-1968

- •
- Sweden
- 19-11-1946

- •
- Switzerland
- 10-09-2002

- •
- Syrian Arab Republic[*]
- 24-10-1945

- T

- Tajikistan
- 02-03-1992

- Thailand
- 16-12-1946

- The former Yugoslav
  Republic of
  Macedonia[*]
- 08-04-1993

- Timor-Leste
- 27-09-2002

- Togo
- 20-09-1960

- Tonga
- 14-09-1999

- Trinidad and Tobago
- 18-09-1962

- Tunisia
- 12-11-1956

- Turkey
- 24-10-1945

- Turkmenistan
- 02-03-1992

- Tuvalu
- 05-09-2000

- U

- Uganda
- 25-10-1962

- Ukraine
- 24-10-1945

- United Arab Emirates

- 09-12-1971

- •
- United Kingdom of Great Britain and Northern Ireland
- 24-10-1945

- •
- United Republic of Tanzania[*]
- 14-12-1961

- •
- United States of America
- 24-10-1945

- •
- Uruguay
- 18-12-1945

- •
- Uzbekistan
- 02-03-1992

- •

V

- •

- •
- Vanuatu
- 15-09-1981

- •
- Venezuela, Bolivarian Republic of
- 15-11-1945

- •
- Viet Nam
- 20-09-1977

- •

Y

- •

- •
- Yemen[*]
- 30-09-1947

- • Z
- •

- •
- Zambia
- 01-12-1964

- •
- Zimbabwe
- 25-08-1980

Biography

Gheorghe Cornel Ardelean was born on March 11.1954 in place Macea, Arad Country Romania Graduate of Economic University, Craiova Romania

1979-1989 Economist and Chief Economist and sales Department

In 1990-founding member of the first Parliament of Romania after the Revolution of 1989 in PCNU (Provisional Council of National Unity)

1992 - Independent candidate for deputy in the Romanian Parliament, Chamber of Deputies

1992-1996 Advisor to the Arad Country Council as an independent adviser

1992-1996 President of the Commission trade, tourism, services advise Arad Country Council

1990-2002 Director, manager of private companies wholesale

1980 - Philosopher and author books.

1980 He published 118 books, articles in publications, of which 50 English books and 68 books in Romanian

In 2009 - Member and Coordinator of Department programs, projects and activities of the non-profit. International Organisation Cornel Gheorghe Ardelean (OIAGC)

As a thought on long-term, positive, constructive, open, creative, humanistic, etc. It has a great ability to create so many positive ideas and solutions, constructive, humanist, creative, helpful people to achieve what they want. Thinking and ideas sustain and promote the rights of children, women, all people in the world, positive thinking and ideas, constructive, humanistic, tolerante, progressive, understanding and peace between peoples and nations.